From the Beginning

From the Beginning
The Story of Human Evolution

David Peters

Morrow Junior Books
New York

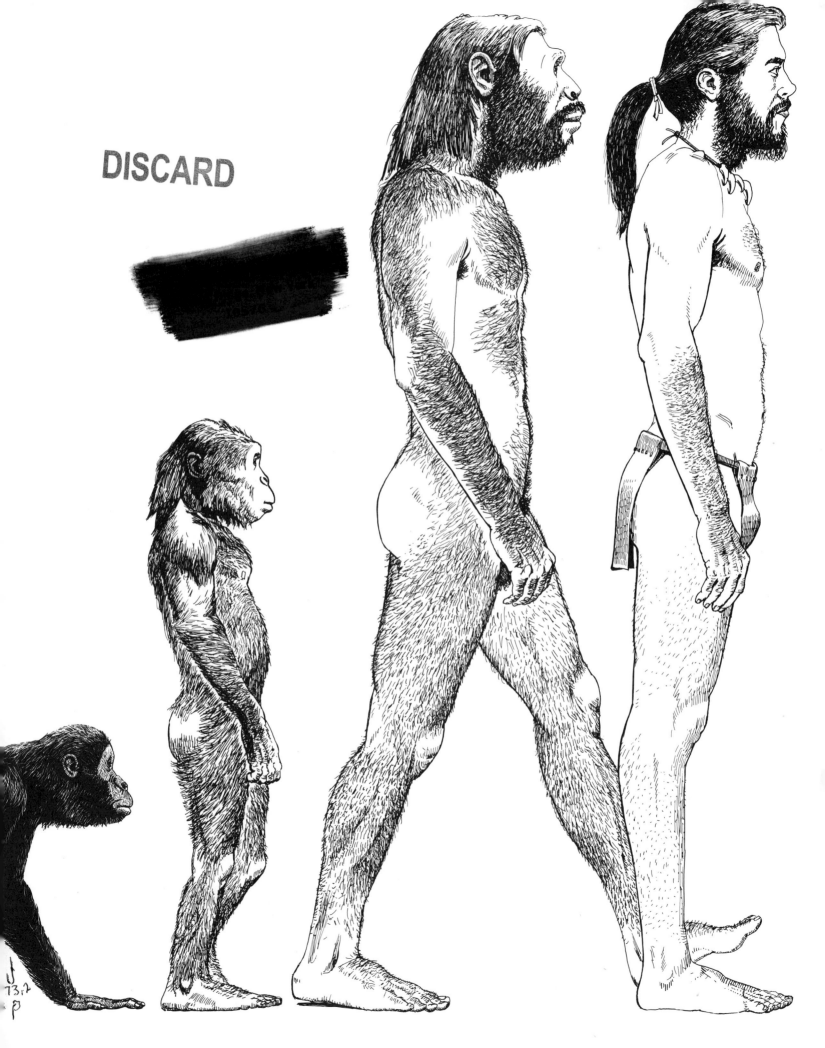

Printed in the United States of America.

1 2 3 4 5 6 7 8 9 10

Library of Congress Cataloging-in-Publication Data
Peters, David, 1954-
From the beginning :
the story of human evolution / David Peters.
p.   cm.
Includes bibliographical references and index.
Summary: Examines the history of
life on Earth and traces the
course of human evolution.
ISBN 0-688-09476-7
1. Human evolution—Juvenile literature.
2. Evolution (Biology)— Juvenile literature.
[1. Evolution.]   I. Title.
GN281.P43   1991
573.2—dc20
90-19187   CIP   AC

Acknowledgments

Mention the word *dinosaur* in a crowd and everyone gets excited. Mention the word *synapsid* in the same crowd and no one knows what you are talking about. They don't even realize that *people* are synapsids, part of a family of animals that includes mammals and a group of reptiles that ruled the earth millions of years before the first dinosaur hatched out of its egg!

In the November 1982 issue of *Science Digest*, nature artist Mark Hallett wrote and illustrated an article entitled, "Class Struggle: The Rise of the Mammal." In that article, Mark introduced his readers to the fascinating world of the synapsids. It was that article that ultimately inspired me to write this book, and for that, Mark, I thank you.

On hearing of my interest in the subject, Mark suggested I contact Dr. James Hopson of the University of Chicago, considered one of the most important workers in the field of evolution. Jim not only guided my research and proofread this book but also offered me many valuable insights into the puzzles of evolution. For your expertise and generosity, Jim, I thank you.

I also want to express my gratitude to Beverly Kobrin, who suggested that I propose this book to David Reuther, editor-in-chief of Morrow Junior Books; and to David Reuther himself, who believed in the book and helped turn it from an idea into a reality. Special thanks, also, to Richard G. Gallin for his many valuable contributions.

Finally, I wish to thank the individual scientists—too numerous to mention—whose scientific papers were my resources and whose discoveries helped to fill in the gaps once present in the human lineage.

Introduction

You may not think a bird and a fish look alike. That's because most people see only the differences that separate things. A scientist also sees the similarities that unite things.

How is a bird like a fish? Look past the obvious differences and you'll see that each has a head, two eyes, two nostrils, and two jaws. Each has a body with a left side, a right side, and a tail. The parts that help them move (wings, legs, and fins) come in pairs behind their heads and beneath their tails. They also have similar muscles and organs.

For centuries, people believed that a fish is a fish, a bird is a bird, and that's that. But when scientists started examining the living animals and the fossils of dead ones, they began to notice more and more similarities. Gradually, scientists concluded that all living things are related. In other words, they all share a common ancestor that lived long ago, when Earth was a young planet.

Human beings are living things, too, and as such can trace their ancestry back to the first living thing. The fact that humans and animals were not created individually but share a common ancestry was, and continues to be, hard for some people to accept.

The evolution from simple chemicals to complex men and women is the subject of this book. You'll not only discover what your ancestors looked like, but you'll find out where, when, and why the various parts of your own body first appeared. About three dozen living and extinct model ancestors are presented in order of their increasing similarity to humans—from the beginning of time to the present day. Many are direct ancestors; others are only close relatives.

Since this book is about human evolution and neglects the millions of other species that inhabit this planet, it may give the false impression that evolution is a ladder of progress reaching toward a goal. The step-by-step layout of this book regrettably reinforces this false impression; that is why the "family tree" charts are so important. In each chart, the reader can see many of the other directions evolution took in past generations.

Some readers may also get the false impression that evolution has been progressing at a steady rate. Actually, different parts of our body became "modern" at different moments in our prehistory. For instance, we have had five fingers and five toes for 360 million years, but our chins appeared less than half a million years ago.

Following a common practice in *anthropology* (the study of apes and humans), nicknames have been given to most of the primates in this book. Similarly, the long scientific names of most of the other animals have been shortened to read more like common names. This has been done simply to make the names easier to read, not to give the animals personalities.

How does evolution work? At one time, people thought the giraffe had acquired a long neck from stretching toward the highest branches. Actually, evolution works the other way around. A giraffe eats from the highest branches because it already *has* a long neck—inherited from its parents. If the opposite were true, then body builders would have muscle-bound babies!

In actuality, each new generation inherits its general characteristics—including body type, size, intelligence, coloration, and aggressiveness—from one or both of its parents. Yet each individual varies to some extent from others of its kind and, if it reproduces, may pass its traits on to a new generation.

Which individuals will live long enough to reproduce is often a matter of luck. In the wild, only a few tadpoles are lucky enough to escape their hungry enemies, mature, and reproduce. But certain widely varying factors seem to increase an individual's luck. Every living thing has some sort of special feature or ability that has helped it to survive as a species. Some are able to climb trees to escape their enemies while others can burrow in the seafloor. Some produce thousands of eggs, thus increasing the chance that some of their offspring will survive.

The Family Tree of Life

The Fossil Record

If every living thing had left a record of its passing, the fossil record would look like a bush. At this time, however, the fossil record looks like a "connect-the-dots" game. Recently, scientists have been able to figure out how most of the dots are connected to one another.

Even a small edge in strength, speed, or agility can be multiplied over many generations into a large advantage. Many fish try to escape predators by leaping out of the water. With their enlarged fins, flying fish excel at this.

The ancestors that had slightly larger flying fins were able to escape while their relatives were being eaten.

However, the characteristics and abilities that helped a species survive in the past may not be as well suited for changing conditions. Rivers may dry up, or a new predator may appear on the scene. If the animal cannot handle the change, it may die without leaving descendants.

Dandelions are an illustration of how nature selects certain features and discards others. In the wild, tall dandelions have a better chance of attracting bees and spreading their seed over a wide area. But on a suburban lawn, mowers select *against* tall dandelions: Only short dandelions escape the blade and thus are able to produce seed. On well-trimmed lawns, tall dandelions soon become extinct while short ones survive. Most of the offspring of shorties inherit this trait from their parents. But there is always some variety. If the seeds of short dandelions drift over to an area that is never mowed, tall dandelions will eventually reappear.

Human beings evolved from a long series of lucky circumstances. Each individual ancestor had the qualities necessary to survive and reproduce within its environment. Changes in this environment were met with corresponding changes in the human body, changes that helped us adapt to the new environment. We humans are the end result of an unbroken chain of parents extending back to that first glimmer of life in a warm pond.

This book is intended to open your eyes, to invite you to observe what all living things have in common. Turtles and pigeons, earthworms and chimps—all have at least some characteristics in common. We are, indeed, all related to one another and to our past.

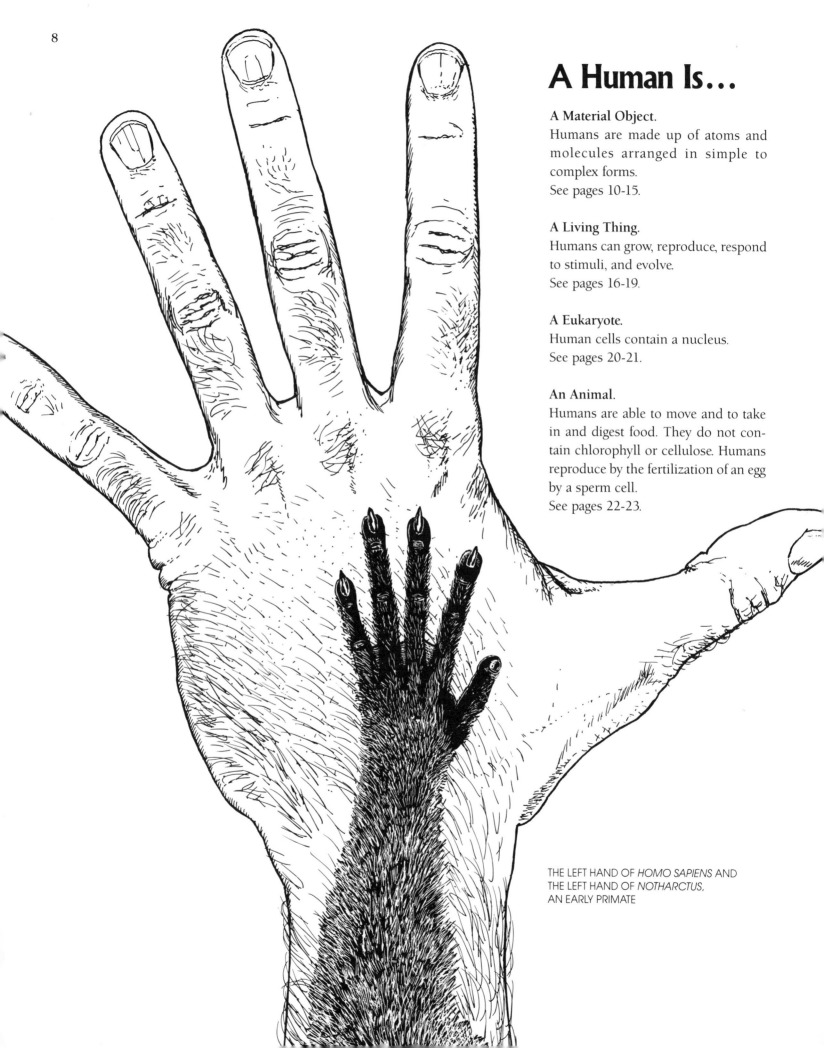

A Human Is...

A Material Object.
Humans are made up of atoms and molecules arranged in simple to complex forms.
See pages 10-15.

A Living Thing.
Humans can grow, reproduce, respond to stimuli, and evolve.
See pages 16-19.

A Eukaryote.
Human cells contain a nucleus.
See pages 20-21.

An Animal.
Humans are able to move and to take in and digest food. They do not contain chlorophyll or cellulose. Humans reproduce by the fertilization of an egg by a sperm cell.
See pages 22-23.

THE LEFT HAND OF *HOMO SAPIENS* AND THE LEFT HAND OF *NOTHARCTUS*, AN EARLY PRIMATE

A Metazoan.
Humans are made up of many different kinds of cells. They are highly dependent on one another and are arranged in definite tissue layers. After fertilization, a blastula (a hollow sphere of cells) develops.
See pages 24-25.

A Bilateral.
Humans are the same on the left and the right halves of their bodies.
See pages 26-27.

A Deuterostome.
As the human embryo is formed, the first opening to appear becomes the anus, and the mouth is formed far away from it.
See pages 29-31.

A Eucoelomate.
Humans have an outer cell layer (the skin), an inner cell layer (the digestive tract), and a coelom between them. The coelom (or "cavity") is a space enclosed by a third cell layer in which the muscles, skeleton, and other organs are found.
See pages 32-33.

A Chordate.
Humans have nerve cords in their backs. Human embryos have a notochord and gill slits.
See pages 32-37.

A Craniate.
Humans have a cranium, or skull.
See pages 38-41.

A Vertebrate.
Humans have a backbone of cartilage and bone.
See pages 38-41.

A Gnathostome.
Humans have jaws.
See pages 42-43.

A Choanate.
Humans have nasal passages that lead into their mouths.
See pages 44-49.

A Tetrapod.
Humans have four limbs. Each limb has one bone close to the body, two farther out, and many more at the end, which form wrist/ankle elements and five jointed digits.
See pages 50-55.

An Amniote.
Human embryos are protected by an amniotic membrane.
See pages 56-59.

A Synapsid.
Human skulls have an opening between the braincase and the cheekbone. In addition, the teeth show some variety in size and shape.
See pages 60-65.

A Therapsid.
Humans have an enlarged skull opening above their cheekbones. Their limbs can raise them above a sprawl and each of the outer four digits is nearly equal in length.
See pages 66-69.

A Cynodont.
Humans have no roof of bones over their jaw muscles. They have a secondary palate and wide cheekbones. A double-headed ball-and-socket joint attaches their head to their neck. Humans have incisors that are chisel-shaped and molars that have more than one point or cusp.
See pages 70-77.

A Mammal.
Human females have mammary glands that produce milk to nourish their young. In addition, humans have hair, three middle ear bones, one jawbone, and only two sets of teeth (milk teeth and adult). See pages 78-83.

A Therian.
Human females give birth to live young; they do not lay eggs.
See pages 84-85.

A Eutherian.
Human females have complex placentas and give birth to fully developed young. They do not have pouches.
See pages 86-89.

A Primate.
Humans have grasping hands, elongated limbs, a shortened snout, and forwardly directed eyes.
See pages 90-93.

An Anthropoid.
Humans have rounded skulls to enclose an enlarged brain, flattened faces, well-developed facial muscles, an uncleft upper lip, close-set eyes that look directly forward, fixed external ears, a real hand with a thumb that moves independently of the other fingers, and a flattened nail on every digit.
See pages 94-95.

A Hominoid.
Humans lack tails and have the ability to swing by the hands from branch to branch, with the body dangling below. The chest is wider than deep, the backbone relatively short and stiff, and the molars have five cusps.
See pages 96-97.

A Hominid.
Humans stand erect and the big toe is aligned with the other toes for walking, not grasping. The canine teeth are not larger than the others.
See pages 98-105.

A Hominine (genus *Homo*).
Humans have greatly enlarged brains.
See pages 106-107.

Of the species *Homo sapiens*.
Humans have reduced brow ridges and high foreheads.
See pages 108-109.

Of the subspecies *Homo sapiens sapiens*.
Humans have a dome-shaped skull, a protruding nose, a chin, and the ability to speak.
See pages 110-113.

The universe started off with a "Big Bang." It was called the Big Bang because the universe has been expanding like the sound waves of an explosion ever since. No one knows what caused the Big Bang. We only know that before it happened, nothing we can measure existed—not time, space, energy, or matter.

Suddenly, the universe existed, and its clock started ticking about 15 billion years ago.

At first, it was far too hot for matter to exist, so pure energy filled the universe. As the universe kept expanding, its energy spread thinner and thinner. Its temperature began to cool. When it cooled down to several millions of degrees, matter appeared. It first appeared as the particles that make up atoms and then, with further cooling, as atoms themselves. The universe is still cooling. Today the temperature of space is 450 degrees below zero Fahrenheit.

Hydrogen and helium are the simplest elements in the universe. These gases make balloons and zeppelins rise because they are lighter than air. The universe today is made up chiefly of hydrogen and helium. In the beginning, however, the universe was made up entirely of these two gases.

Stars are mainly great concentrations of hydrogen and helium that have been condensed and compacted by the force of gravity. Gravity is a little-understood force of attraction that acts between every atom in the universe. It increases with mass (the amount of matter) and decreases with distance, but regardless of mass or distance, it is always present.

In the early universe the feeble but far-reaching effects of gravity attracted hydrogen and helium atoms to mass together and condense into clouds. These clouds attracted other clouds. They didn't remain wispy clouds for long. The force of gravity produced clouds with a condensed core, proto-stars.

As the space between atoms in a proto-star decreased, the atoms chanced to hit each other more often. Before long they were bouncing off each other like lotto balls. Each

THE ORIGIN OF TIME AND MATTER

bounce created a little bit of heat energy. The denser the gas became, the hotter it got. In the end, these lighter-than-air gases were compressed until they became denser than any metal. The atoms were in a frenzy and the temperature soared.

When the proto-star's core temperature rose to 20 million degrees Fahrenheit, something extraordinary happened. The hydrogen atoms stopped bouncing off one another and began to fuse together. By fusing they became helium, and in the process, transformed a tiny part of their matter into a tremendous amount of energy. (The fusion of hydrogen atoms also powers H-bombs.)

When the energy from the core finally reached the surface of the proto-star, it caused the gases there to give off light. A ball of gas that produces its own light is a star. Gravity ignites a star and keeps it burning.

Billions of stars usually form in vast clusters known as galaxies, such as our own Milky Way galaxy.

A star begins to die when its supply of hydrogen runs out. The energy radiating from the core dies down, and gravity, that ever-present force, pulls more matter into the core. This raises the core's temperature so high that helium atoms begin to fuse into yet heavier elements, such as carbon. When the supply of helium is exhausted, carbon and other heavy elements fuse into still heavier elements, such as oxygen. That is how the 92 naturally occurring elements of chemistry are formed. Gravity and fusion "cook" them within the interiors of stars.

As a star dies, bursts of energy, like flash fires in the core, can literally blow it to pieces. A supernova is a star explosion so spectacular that it can outshine an entire galaxy for several days. At the same time, the explosion sends star-matter back into space. This is the way that heavy elements, such as carbon, oxygen, gold, and lead, are shot out into space. These elements, along with hydrogen and helium gas clouds, then become raw material to make new stars and rocky planets, such as Earth.

Our own galaxy, the Milky Way, is about 11 billion years old. Not long after it began, star-matter from a number of supernovas began to cloud up in our part of the Milky Way. Five billion years ago, our own star, the Sun, began to condense from within one of these clouds of matter.

When it became dense enough and hot enough, the Sun ignited. Orbiting farther out were the planets, formed from much smaller whirlpool eddies of matter.

As the largest clump in its vicinity, Earth soon attracted and swept up much of the rest of the gas, dust, and smaller clumps in its path. Only the Moon escaped by falling into a stable orbit around the planet.

About 4.5 billion years ago, Earth was a red-hot seething cauldron resembling the inside of a volcano. It had been heated from above by bombarding space-matter and from below by the force of gravity. No earth-rocks remain from this period, aptly labeled the Hadean era (after Hades, the mythological land of the dead).

After hundreds of millions of years, the bombardment of Earth slowed. Earth's surface temperature began to drop as it lost its heat to the chill of space. The Moon, with less mass,

THE BIRTH OF THE SOLAR SYSTEM

cooled more quickly. The craters on its surface were made during this era. They are a permanent record of the chaotic Hadean era.

About 3.9 billion years ago a thin, more or less permanent crust developed on Earth. This marked the beginning of the Archean (or "ancient") era. Still, Earth remained a hot and violent place. It spun on its axis once every ten hours. Volcanoes, together with cracks in the crust, released Earth's inner heat. They spewed ashes, lava, water vapor, carbon dioxide, and poisonous gases into the sky. Gases were released when rock melted deep inside Earth. In contrast to the Moon, Earth had enough gravity to keep its gaseous atmosphere from drifting off into space.

Soon, the crust cooled below the boiling point of water. Storm clouds rained for decades. Lightning lit up the sky. As the years passed, water filled the valleys and basins. In time, the great oceans were formed. Rain-water trickling across the land picked up minerals and salts. The sea became salty. Erosion smoothed out Earth's crater-pocked surface.

Billions of years had passed since the beginning of time. On this little planet in the vast universe, it had finally become wet enough and warm enough for lifeless atoms to begin assembling themselves into the complex chemicals that would someday become living matter.

A SHORT HISTORY OF THE COSMOS

TIME BEGINS • STARS FIRST APPEAR   SUN IGNITES • • EARTH FORMS • LIFE APPEARS   HUMANS •

14 BILLION   12 BILLION   10 BILLION   8 BILLION   6 BILLION   4 BILLION   2 BILLION   TODAY

Chemical Evolution—it starts with atoms that are naturally

HYDROGEN
2 atoms
hydrogen
H_2

WATER
2 atoms
hydrogen
1 atom
oxygen
H_2O

AMMONIA
3 atoms
hydrogen
1 atom
nitrogen
NH_3

METHANE
4 atoms
hydrogen
1 atom
carbon
CH_4

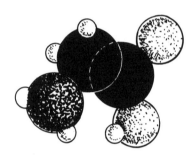

GLYCINE (an amino acid)
5 atoms hydrogen
1 atom nitrogen
2 atoms oxygen
2 atoms carbon
$CH_2(NH_2)COOH$

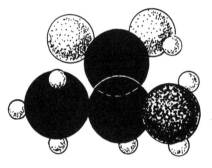

ALANINE (an amino acid)
7 atoms hydrogen
1 atom nifrogen
2 atoms oxygen
3 atoms carbon
$CH_3CH(NH_2)COOH$

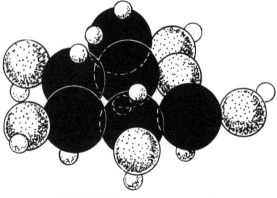

GLUCOSE (a simple sugar)
12 atoms hydrogen
6 atoms oxygen
6 atoms carbon
$C_6H_{12}O_6$

Molecules come in a variety of sizes and shapes depending entirely on the atoms from which they are made. In the above illustration, each sphere represents one atom. Molecules containing at least one carbon atom are termed *organic molecules*. Except for water, every molecule in every living thing has at least one carbon atom. As seen in the illustration above, simple sugars and amino acids are not very complex. The most abundant amino acids in the human body are also the easiest for nature to produce. Proteins are complex because they are built from thousands of amino acids put together in very specific patterns that are difficult to unravel or duplicate.

Earth and the universe are made of matter. Matter is made up of various combinations of elements. There are only 92 elements that occur naturally. Oxygen, gold, and carbon are well-known examples.

Elements are made up of atoms. An atom is the smallest particle of an element that still behaves like the element of which it is a part.

Atoms, in turn, are made up of subatomic particles. The three important ones are protons, neutrons, and electrons. The number of protons in an atom determines which element it is. Hydrogen, for example, has 1 proton, helium has 2, lithium has 3, and so on.

Nature uses only 6 elements to make up 99 percent of all living matter. These 6 are hydrogen, oxygen, carbon, nitrogen, sulfur, and phosphorus.

Molecules are combinations of atoms. Chemicals are combinations of elements or the elements themselves. Atoms usually look and behave quite differently when joined with others, and of course, the combinations are endless. Water is a molecule made of 2 atoms of hydrogen and 1 atom of oxygen. It looks and behaves differently from the way either element does alone.

Molecules do not form randomly but in ordered, patterned ways. In water, for example, each molecule is lopsided because the two hydrogen atoms always line up on one side of the oxygen atom at a 105-degree angle from one another. Without the natural attraction certain atoms have for one another and the precise patterns in which they align themselves, life itself would not be possible. Molecules are like a puzzle with interlocking pieces.

Shortly after Earth's crust solidified and its surface cooled to just below

attractive.

water's boiling point, rainwater began filling in the low spots. As it fell, rain picked up carbon dioxide, nitrogen, hydrogen, and sulfur from the atmosphere. As this chemical solution splashed on the rocks, it dissolved more elements. The highlands eroded. Their sediments slowly settled in the lowlands. Sands and clays formed from matter that settled out of floodwaters.

Evaporation during droughts concentrated clays and the other rainwater chemicals in mud-flat puddles near the sea. The result was a gooey sludge at the water's edge. Sunlight and lightning bolts zapped the sludge. The simple elements within banded together to form a variety of more complex chemicals based on carbon, such as amino acids and simple sugars.

In time, numbers of amino acids and sugars linked together to form long, complex chain molecules called proteins. Today, proteins make up a large part of the substance in each living cell. Proteins also act as enzymes to hasten chemical reactions.

The origin of life from simple elements could not have taken place without clay. Clay was the base on which the chains of amino acids slowly assembled into proteins. Clay is formed of microscopic crystals, usually of irregular and complex shape. These shapes continue growing in layers as more clay crystallizes on their surface. Each new layer "inherits" the shape of the one below it. As changes occur, the crystals "evolve." Those early amino acids that existed within the framework of clay crystals also inherited the patterns of previous layers. When they finally formed certain patterns, some of these amino-acid chains became proteins.

With complex proteins being formed and held in position on clay, life itself was just around the corner.

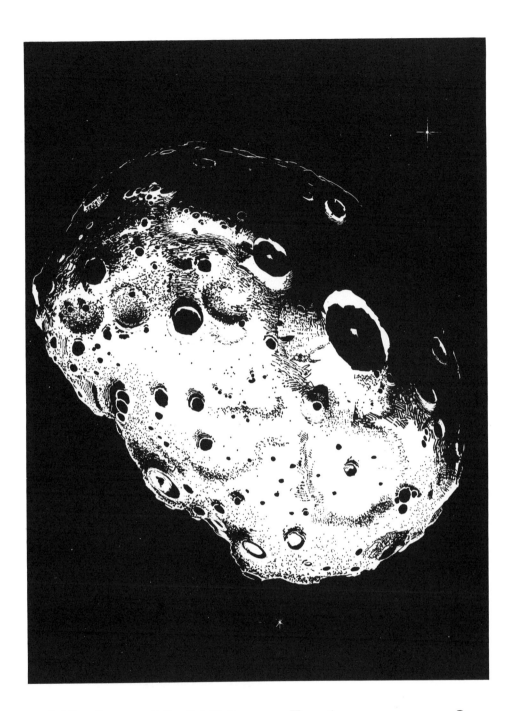

Life-forms hitchhiking to Earth on meteors?

As anyone knows who has seen weeds growing from cracks in concrete, life will spring forth wherever it is given even half a chance to do so. Amino acids and other organic chemicals found in human cells have also been found on meteorites and comets exposed for aeons to the hazards of space. Some say that meteors brought life to this barren planet. It is more likely, however, that early Earth had just as many amino acids as any meteor did. All the matter in this solar system came together at the same time and under roughly the same conditions. Lucky for us, Earth was just wet enough and warm enough for complex chemicals to become living chemicals.

DNA (Deoxyribonucleic Acid)—the blueprint of life.

On this tiny portion of a DNA molecular strand, each sphere represents one atom. The molecular rungs that hold this ladder together determine the design of proteins in living things. Some proteins will produce body parts, others will produce body chemicals.

Every living cell has architects and builders, the way buildings do. These architects and builders construct complex body chemicals and body parts from the simple chemicals provided.

DNA is the architect's file cabinet. It contains detailed plans for building proteins and other cell substances that have worked successfully in the past. It is a giant molecule made up of amino acids. It is shaped like a spiraling ladder with hundreds of thousands of molecular "rungs." Despite the huge number of rungs, there are only four types. Their plan is coded in the sequence of their appearance across a long series in the ladder. In this way, the language of DNA creates very complex "words" with an "alphabet" of only four "letters."

The plans have to be delivered from the architect to the builder. Messenger RNA, a simpler cousin of DNA, makes the delivery. RNA reshapes itself to become a chemical mold of the DNA pattern. It then delivers the mold of the plan to the cell's protein builder, the ribosome.

Along with plans, a builder needs raw materials. The amino acids used to build the proteins are also delivered to the ribosomes by smaller RNA molecules. Then construction begins. One by one, the various amino acids line up along the entire length of the messenger RNA mold. In doing so, they become the long protein chain called for by the original DNA plan. Its work finished, the RNA molecule breaks free from the completed protein to begin the task again. The entire process lasts from a few seconds to a few minutes.

The earliest DNA molecules must have been much shorter and simpler than any known today. They may have copied less well and made errors more often.

A DNA molecule with one of its rungs in error is like a record with a scratch in it. When re-recorded on a tape, the sound of the scratch remains. In DNA, the error produces new proteins, which lead to new body chemistry or structures called mutations. Will the mutation prove good or bad? That depends on circumstances, but most mutations, such as birth defects, are disasters. A wasp without wings will probably die, but ants have evolved from wasps that have lost their wings.

Mutations usually affect only one gene, or that portion of a DNA molecule responsible for a specific characteristic. Eye color, for example, is determined by a single gene.

In addition to physical traits, "mental" traits are also inherited by way of DNA. That is why some humans are naturally more aggressive or athletic than others. That is also why some have a talent for mathematics or music. Humans are basically the same all around the world, but not one is exactly the same as another.

In the cell (see page 16), DNA molecules are usually found lined up by the thousands, creating a threadlike structure called a chromosome. Each DNA molecule has a specific place in line. Bacteria have one chromosome, humans have forty-six. Some animals have more.

DNA molecules have the ability to reproduce themselves (see illustration), something no other molecule can do. With the first appearance of primitive DNA molecules in moist clay, life had its origin (see page 16).

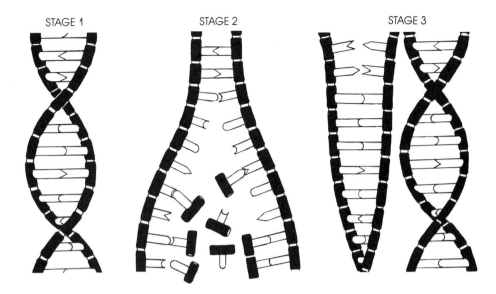

STAGE 1   STAGE 2   STAGE 3

REPRODUCTION IN DNA

DNA reproduces itself by slowly unzipping at one end, each molecular "rung" breaking apart in the middle. Each broken rung acts as a template that recombines only with a freely floating molecule identical to its previous bonding partner. In this way, rung by rung, each half of the ladder rebuilds its missing half exactly. In the end, this produces two identical strands of DNA where only one had been before.

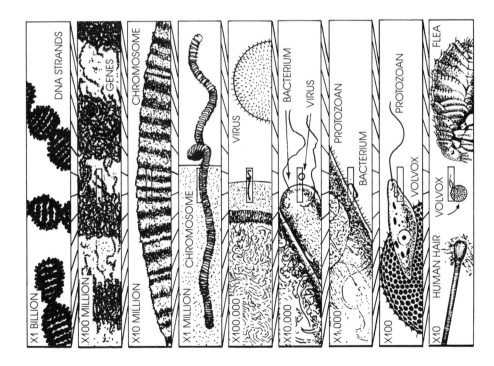

THE SCALE OF LIVING THINGS

Each illustration above is a tenfold enlargement of the central area of the one to its right. Each is labeled with the objects that fill the view and the scale at which they are viewed. In this way, one can compare the size of an atom on a DNA molecule to the size of a human hair, and everything in between. The chemistry of life exists on an exceedingly small scale. For the first nine-tenths of Earth's history, no living thing grew larger than the items pictured above.

The Origin of Life—bacteria are more than just germs.

Only a living thing can absorb nutrients and grow, reproduce on its own, respond to stimuli, and evolve. When the clay-based concentration of amino acids was finally able to perform all four functions by itself, by definition it became alive.

Living things are a part of this world, yet each living thing is a world unto itself. The barrier between each living thing and the world at large is the cell membrane. It is a wrapping that encloses the basic unit of life, the cell. When cells became packaged in cell membranes, they were free to float off their clay base and continue living elsewhere.

Cell membranes are composed of fatty carbon and phosphorus compounds called lipids. Like oil droplets in water, lipids tend to form round drops and bubbles. Surrounding the cell, a lipid membrane allows certain substances, such as nutrients, to enter while it keeps others out.

Even before life had officially begun, nutrient molecules from the outside had been admitted and added to the interior structure. Waste molecules had been expelled. The cell began to grow. When the fragile lipid-bubble membrane grew too large to remain in one piece, it divided neatly in two. Surface tension, the same force that makes drops out of falling water, kept the two halves intact. This humble beginning was the start of cellular reproduction.

Once started, reproduction never stopped. Those tiny sacs of simple nucleic acids continued to absorb beneficial atoms from the seawater that continually washed in. The cells grew and divided until they covered the sea and other wet areas with life. These were early forms of bacteria, the simplest and most primitive living

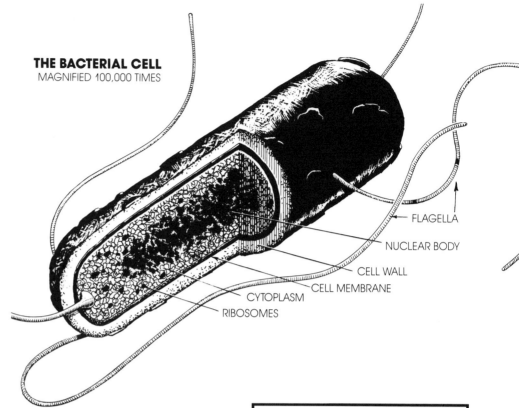

THE BACTERIAL CELL
MAGNIFIED 100,000 TIMES

— FLAGELLA
— NUCLEAR BODY
— CELL WALL
— CELL MEMBRANE
— CYTOPLASM
— RIBOSOMES

things known.

A bacterium is little more than a cellular membrane with a strand of DNA and seawatery cytoplasm inside it. Cytoplasm is the salty, organically rich liquid bath in which the strand of DNA floats.

The fossil remains of bacteria date back 3.5 billion years. Even today many types exist only in hot springs or sulfur pits similar to Earth's earliest environments.

As we have seen, reproduction is the way in which bacteria deal with excess cellular material. It takes place when the cell has ingested so much, it has to divide in two. This is called fission. Under ideal conditions, fission can take place as often as every fifteen to thirty minutes. It results in two identical cells. Mutations occur once every million divisions, on the average. Sometimes bacteria do not completely

What's New?

Life
The cell, including the plasma
membrane, cytoplasm, ribosomes
and one strand of DNA
Sex
Fermentation
Respiration
Photosynthesis

disconnect but form long filaments, like beads on a string.

In plants and animals, sex precedes reproduction, but originally sex and reproduction had nothing to do with each other. Sex is the joining, by whatever means, of two separate sets of genetic material. Among bacteria, DNA is shared, exchanged, ingested, and absorbed. Bacteria may even be infected with the DNA of others by way of a virus. After receiving this new genetic information, a bacterium's

The Bacterial Cell

At its simplest, the cell is composed of an elastic cell membrane made of lipids that encloses a nuclear body and cytoplasm. The nuclear body is a single bunched-up chromosome, usually containing fewer than 3,000 genes. That is not really very many sets of instructions for fulfilling every one of the functions of a living thing.

Most bacteria also have a tough outer cell wall. Sometimes protein filaments, called flagella, project from the surface and whip about, pushing the cell from place to place. Ribosomes are the giant molecules where proteins are manufactured.

internal chemistry is usually changed. It can be said to have evolved during its own lifetime. For example, during sex a bacterium may receive the genes that give it immunity to certain medicines. It can share this immunity with other bacteria in a network that can often range worldwide, given enough time.

Despite appearances to the contrary, some bacteria are as different from one another chemically as they are from higher organisms. Two major groups survive to this day. Archaebacteria, or "ancient bacteria," all live in extreme environments or have peculiar food requirements. Eubacteria, or "true bacteria," live in more common environments. Both groups are equally ancient, and both have contributed chemistry to the cells of all plants and animals (see page 20).

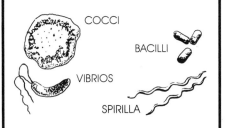

Visible Variation in Bacteria

Scientists sometimes divide bacteria according to shape. Cocci are round, bacilli are rod-shaped, and vibrios are bent in the middle. Spirilla (spirochetes) are corkscrew-shaped. In most cases, shape has little to do with the internal makeup of the bacterium, which is a much more important characteristic.

Is a virus a living thing?

A virus is a single RNA or DNA molecule surrounded by a protein coating. Usually it is much smaller than the smallest bacterium, measuring only about one-millionth of an inch across. A virus fails our definition of a life-form because it lacks the ability to reproduce on its own. It requires a host cell.

VIRUS

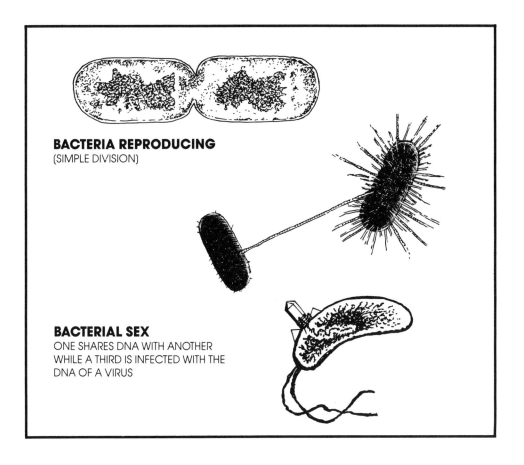

BACTERIA REPRODUCING
(SIMPLE DIVISION)

BACTERIAL SEX
ONE SHARES DNA WITH ANOTHER WHILE A THIRD IS INFECTED WITH THE DNA OF A VIRUS

The Long History of Bacteria—the true masters of Earth.

When life first began, the sea was full of sugars, amino acids, and other biological chemicals that had not yet become living things. These organic molecules, called the "primordial soup," may have originally made up 10 percent of the volume of the entire sea. The very first bacteria simply absorbed these molecules as they were needed. As these primitive bacteria began eating, they began multiplying. It was not long before the sea was thick with primitive bacteria and they had eaten the last of their "soup." Famine swept through the seas in Earth's first major extinction event.

All was not lost, however. Because of mutation, there are always a few bacteria that are able to survive almost any situation. Varieties appeared that were suited to new diets.

Shortly before the first famine occurred, some varieties of primitive bacteria had evolved the ability to ferment, or break down, complex carbon-based molecules into the simple food molecules once found in the primordial soup.

Fermentation allowed bacteria to ingest their dead comrades. Ever since, bacteria have been keeping Earth clean and tidy by recycling the organic chemicals of dead things in a process called decay.

Some food takers became food makers. They survived by being able to synthesize their own food molecules from simpler substances. Some types made food from common compounds in seawater and air. Others made food from bacterial waste products. This process must have taken place gradually, because, even today, some organisms can make some, but not all, of what they require. Some bacteria used the heat from hot springs as their energy source. Others,

called photosynthetic bacteria, used the Sun.

Sunlight killed the first bacteria. But photosynthetic bacteria *required* it. Ultraviolet or UV light is a part of sunlight that is particularly harmful to living things. It breaks down fragile chemical bonds. In high enough doses, UV light sunburns human skin. Some forms of photosynthetic bacteria survived by developing chemicals called pigments that absorbed the harmful rays. Others lived in the shade.

Shade was created by floating mats of photosynthetic bacteria known as blue-green algae. In some localities, these mat colonies became embedded with dissolved minerals. After decades, layer upon layer of these minerals shaped rocky mounds, known today as stromatolites. Stromatolites are the most ancient fossils the naked eye can see. Today stromatolites form only in lagoons where it is too salty for bacteria-eating organisms to live.

Between 2.2 and 1.8 billion years ago, photosynthetic bacteria grew throughout the world. The waste product of photosynthesis is the gas oxygen. As stromatolites spread, oxygen levels in the atmosphere rose from one part in a million to today's level of one part in five.

Most of Earth's fermenting bacteria were poisoned by oxygen. This created yet another worldwide extinction event. But just as certain bacteria had grown tolerant of sunlight, certain bacteria also became tolerant of oxygen.

Others developed a cell chemistry that actually *required* oxygen. Respiring, or oxygen burning, releases energy from food many times more efficiently than does fermentation.

Certain bacteria combined photosynthesis and respiration. By both making oxygen and using it, they became well adapted to this gas.

With the introduction of oxygen into the atmosphere, a type of oxygen called ozone also appeared. In the upper atmosphere it formed a layer that acted to filter out much of the harmful UV light coming in. As those damaging rays lessened, life was finally able to come out of the shade.

The evolution of cells more complex than simple bacteria probably came about through symbiosis. Symbiotic organisms are unrelated living things that live together for their mutual good. Eukaryotes, or cells with a nucleus (see page 20), were composed of several different types of independent bacterial cells. After being joined together, they could not live without each other.

The original bacterial symbiosis probably occurred when bacteria without flagella acted as hosts to spirochetes, the speedsters of the bacterial world. These corkscrew-shaped bacteria have their flagella on the inside, so their whole body twists and spins while swimming. Whenever they gang up on a host, they usually feed on the surface with their tails beating in unison. The host cell, while being consumed, is pushed around from place to place.

Evidently, certain giant host cells were large enough to sustain a spirochete attack and still keep feeding even though they were being eaten at the same time. Swimming in unison, the spirochetes kept their host well fed by moving it into food-rich areas.

Other eukaryote cell parts enter the picture at later dates.

The History of Life on Earth

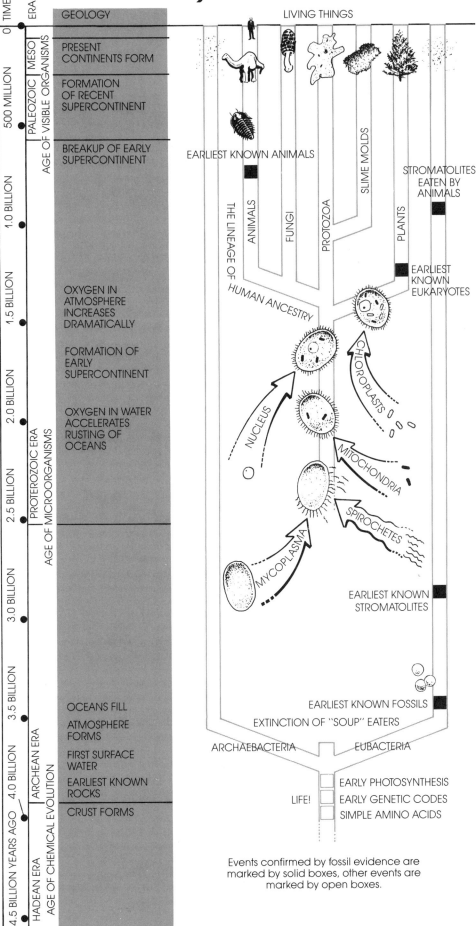

LIVING THINGS

TIME	ERA	GEOLOGY

0 TIME

PRESENT CONTINENTS FORM — PALEOZOIC / MESO — AGE OF VISIBLE ORGANISMS

FORMATION OF RECENT SUPERCONTINENT — 500 MILLION

BREAKUP OF EARLY SUPERCONTINENT — 1.0 BILLION

EARLIEST KNOWN ANIMALS

THE LINEAGE OF HUMAN ANCESTRY

ANIMALS · FUNGI · PROTOZOA · SLIME MOLDS · PLANTS

STROMATOLITES EATEN BY ANIMALS

OXYGEN IN ATMOSPHERE INCREASES DRAMATICALLY — 1.5 BILLION

EARLIEST KNOWN EUKARYOTES

FORMATION OF EARLY SUPERCONTINENT

OXYGEN IN WATER ACCELERATES RUSTING OF OCEANS — 2.0 BILLION

NUCLEUS · CHLOROPLASTS · MITOCHONDRIA · SPIROCHETES · MYCOPLASMA

2.5 BILLION — PROTEROZOIC ERA — AGE OF MICROORGANISMS

EARLIEST KNOWN STROMATOLITES

3.0 BILLION

3.5 BILLION

OCEANS FILL

ATMOSPHERE FORMS

EARLIEST KNOWN FOSSILS

EXTINCTION OF "SOUP" EATERS

FIRST SURFACE WATER

4.0 BILLION — ARCHEAN ERA

ARCHAEBACTERIA · EUBACTERIA

EARLIEST KNOWN ROCKS

CRUST FORMS

LIFE! — EARLY PHOTOSYNTHESIS / EARLY GENETIC CODES / SIMPLE AMINO ACIDS

4.5 BILLION YEARS AGO — HADEAN ERA — AGE OF CHEMICAL EVOLUTION

Events confirmed by fossil evidence are marked by solid boxes, other events are marked by open boxes.

Bacteria prepare a planet for higher forms of life and they are the only forms of life capable of maintaining a living planet. Some scientists knew that Mars would prove to be a dead planet because bacteria had not created very much oxygen in its thin atmosphere. No other planet in our system has an atmosphere like the Earth's. It seems as if there are no other living planets in the Solar System. Perhaps atmospheric sampling will be our first clue to finding life on planets orbiting other stars.

Although the most famous bacteria are those which produce diseases, the great majority of bacteria are helpful, not harmful. Some kinds change milk into cheese and yogurt. Other types change fruit, vegetable, and grain juices into alcoholic beverages, such as wine and beer.

Certain bacteria take nitrogen from the air and release it as a chemical compound similar to ammonia as a waste product. Animals and plants cannot take nitrogen directly from the atmosphere, but they can use this nitrogen compound waste product. In fact they need it. Nitrogen-using bacteria are, therefore, absolutely essential for our continuing existence.

Some bacteria decay other organisms. Without them, dead things would never "disappear". Dead things don't stink. It is the waste gas of these bacteria that smells bad.

Mothers always remind us to wash because bacteria are always present on human skin. What mothers don't tell you is that bacteria are necessary to keep in check the fungi that settle on us throughout the day. An excess of bacteria kept moist with sweat is what leads to body odor, particularly in old sneakers.

Eukaryotes—bacterial corporations in the "nuclear" age.

All living things other than bacteria are eukaryotes. A eukaryote (meaning "true kernel" or "nucleus") is a living thing with a nucleus in each cell.

Surrounded by its own membrane, the nucleus is a spherical structure containing DNA arranged in strands of chromosomes. Therefore, most of the cell's genetic information and protein-making instructions come from this organelle (or "tiny organ"). Smaller bodies, called nucleoli, may also be included in a nucleus. These provide sites for making ribosomes, the protein-manufacturing organelles within each and every living cell.

Eukaryotes are vastly different from bacteria. Their protein chemistry is different, the cytoplasm is always in motion, and the cell is subdivided by a series of internal canals. Last but not least, each of the component parts of a eukaryote is contained within its own membrane.

A typical eukaryote cell is likely to be 10 times longer than a bacterium and 1,000 times its volume. The typical number of DNA molecules in a eukaryote also rises by a factor of 1,000, bringing the total number into the millions.

How eukaryotes may have evolved from symbiotic bacteria is introduced on pages 18-19. Experiments have shown that predatory bacteria, under certain conditions, can turn from being harmful to their prey to becoming a part of their prey. Eventually they may become essential to their former prey's survival, all within five years in a laboratory.

The home, or host, for all the organelles, including the nucleus, is the cell itself. Something like *Thermoplasma*, a type of bacteria lacking a cell wall, probably served as the original host. Among bacteria, only this type has certain chemicals also seen in plants and animals. Today *Thermoplasma* lives in hot coals and scalding springs where the temperature hovers at 140 degrees Fahrenheit and the acidity is equal to that of concentrated sulfuric acid. These environments are similar to that of early Earth. Oxygen-respiring predators came to live within these wall-less cells. They provided their host with the energy and ability to live in cooler and less acidic areas.

The origin of the nucleus remains unclear. Perhaps a large host engulfed a smaller bacterium that went on to become its nucleus. Perhaps the host's own DNA wrapped itself within a membrane. In either case, whenever that happened, the host cell became a eukaryote.

The eukaryote cell organelles with the task of respiring energy for the rest of the cell are called mitochondria (my-toe-KON-dree-uh). At one time they, too, were probably independent bacteria. They are similar in size, shape, and chemistry to certain eubacteria (see pages 16-17). They have their own DNA and divide independently of their home cells.

On the surface of some eukaryote cells are small cell whips known as cilia and large ones known as flagella (not to be confused with bacterial flagella, see pages 16-17). Whether large or small, eukaryote cell whips seem to be former spirochete bacteria. They propel a cell by their waving motion or, if the cell is fixed in place and cup-shaped, they wave food into it.

No matter where cell whips appear, as sperm tails, on protozoans, or in lung lining, they are always made up of the same microtubules. These microtubules are identified by their cross-sectional arrangement of 9 pairs in a circle surrounding 2 single tubules.

Whenever cell division is about to take place, these cell whips disappear inside the main body of the cell. Shortly thereafter, microtubules appear within the cell. They assist in dividing the nucleus and its chromosomes apart and pulling each half into each half of the dividing cell. After cell division is complete, the cell whips reappear again on the outside surface. Because cell whips become absorbed prior to cell division, a eukaryote cell cannot swim and divide at the same time. In humans, some cells have become stuck in either one stage or the other. Fertilized egg cells have no cell whips. Their job is to keep dividing until they produce a baby. Sperm cells, on the other hand, have permanent tails and cannot divide at all. Rods and cones, the highly energized nerve cells specialized for vision, seem to have evolved from cell whips. They, too, cannot divide and are made up for the most part of microtubules in a 9-plus-2 design.

Isn't it fascinating to think that every cell in the human body is composed of formerly independent bacterial cells now living together, each with a special task to do, such as reading this book?

Most of the five senses began with one-celled organisms. Taste and smell are ways to detect traces of chemicals in an environment. One-celled creatures are attracted to the chemical trails of food and mating partners. They are repelled by the smell and taste of predators, poisons, and other harsh environments. Some cells are attracted to light and can sense from which direction it comes. Cells may also sense vibrations in the water; for instance, the beating of cell whips

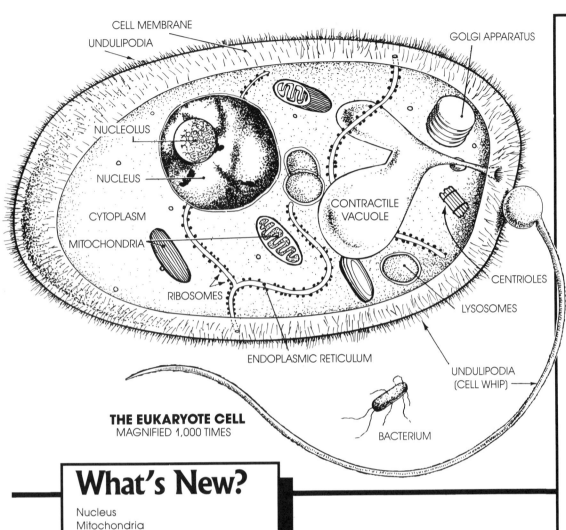

CELL MEMBRANE
UNDULIPODIA
GOLGI APPARATUS
NUCLEOLUS
NUCLEUS
CYTOPLASM
MITOCHONDRIA
RIBOSOMES
CONTRACTILE VACUOLE
CENTRIOLES
LYSOSOMES
ENDOPLASMIC RETICULUM
UNDULIPODIA (CELL WHIP)
BACTERIUM

THE EUKARYOTE CELL
MAGNIFIED 1,000 TIMES

What's New?

Nucleus
Mitochondria
Cell whips
Other cell organelles
Larger overall size
Reproduction occasionally with
   gametes, or sex cells

CELL PARTS

Unlike bacterial cells, eukaryotes are composed of many separately packaged parts. Those not mentioned in the text are described here.

The **endoplasmic reticulum** is the membrane canal system along which ribosomes are located.

Lysosomes are organelles containing a number of different enzymes to break down biological molecules and dispose of worn out cell parts.

The **Golgi apparatus** consist of stacked sacks for packaging proteins and enzymes, such as digestive juices.

Centrioles are bundles of rods connecting microtubules that form during cell division.

The **cell membrane** is the double-walled sack that holds the cell together, separating its contents from the outside world. It also filters nutrients and out-going waste products.

The **contractile vacuole** is a sack inside the cell in which excess water accumulates. When the sack is full, it contracts, expelling the water to the outside of the cell. Other vacuoles develop around food to digest it and finally expel it in a similar fashion.

from neighboring cells.

Eukaryotes developed new ways to reproduce. Some produced spores, tiny cells that grow to become mature cells. Some spores have all the DNA they need as an adult. Others have only half the amount and are known as gametes, or sex cells. In animals, gametes have become specialized as egg and sperm cells. It is necessary for two gametes to meet and combine their DNA in order to have the full amount they need. The resulting sexual union forms a new individual with a unique mix of inherited genes from both parent cells.

The earliest known fossils of eukaryotes are 1.5-billion-year-old algae cysts. It is quite probable, however, that eukaryotes originated some 300 million years earlier than that.

The Blastula—get a bunch of cells together and have a ball.

Sometimes when cells divide, they remain stuck to one another. Sometimes they form a long strand of cells. Other times they form flat mats. A few cell colonies form a blastula (or "little bud"), which is a hollow sphere of from 8 to more than 50,000 cells.

Usually, sticky cells don't communicate with each other. However, animal cells are an exception. The way their cells remain connected to one another makes it possible for them to coordinate their movements. It is as if the cells were all of one mind.

Nowadays there are no animals shaped like hollow spheres. But all animals go through a blastula stage as embryos. It seems likely that this form was at one time the shape of their common ancestor.

On the surface of a hollow sphere, each cell has equal access to nutrients and gases from the outside world. Each cell feeds by itself and dumps its own waste products to the outside. In addition, each cell is defended by other cells on all sides but the outside. With a larger size came a greater resistance to attack from predators. One billion years ago, when blastulas probably originated, there would have been nothing else large enough to eat one whole. As tiny as a pinhead, a blastula would have been the largest animal on Earth up to that time.

Volvocines, a family of microscopic pond weed that exists today, is a living model of the evolution and behavior of animal blastulas.

At first, the most primitive multi-celled creatures had only 2 cells. These split to make 4, then 8, then 16, then 32 cells altogether. Human beings, like all animals, grow this way following fertilization.

At this stage, all the cells remained alike. They made a ball with each one

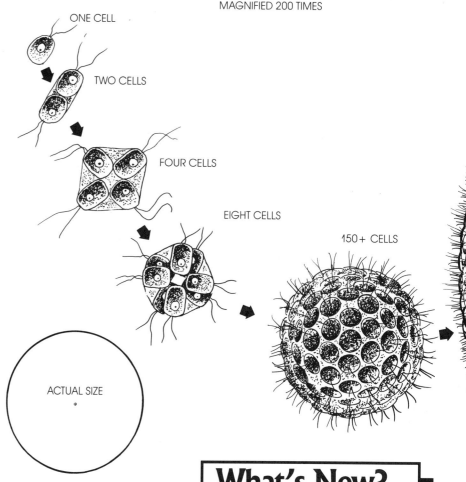

THE DEVELOPMENT AND EVOLUTION OF THE BLASTULA
MAGNIFIED 200 TIMES

ONE CELL

TWO CELLS

FOUR CELLS

EIGHT CELLS

150+ CELLS

ACTUAL SIZE

pointing in toward the center and their wiggling tails (or cell whips) pointing out. A jellylike substance may have kept them stuck to one another. Each individual could have lived and reproduced alone, but their tails beat in unison to keep them all moving in the same direction.

With a slight adjustment, the ball of 32 cells could form into a hollow sphere. In this shape, every neighbor lined up side by side. While swimming, the sphere spun on its axis, like a planet. One particular cell always served as the pole and always pointed in the direction of travel.

What's New?

Multi-celled organization
Inner and outer surfaces
Blastula formation
Tissue specialization
Egg and sperm of vastly different size
   and appearance
Intercellular communication
Birth
Larger overall size

The cells grew dependent on one another. Soon, no cell could live independently or else it would die. This was not a case of symbiosis, because all the cells were alike and related to one another.

The gametes, or sex cells, began to take on their separate roles and were

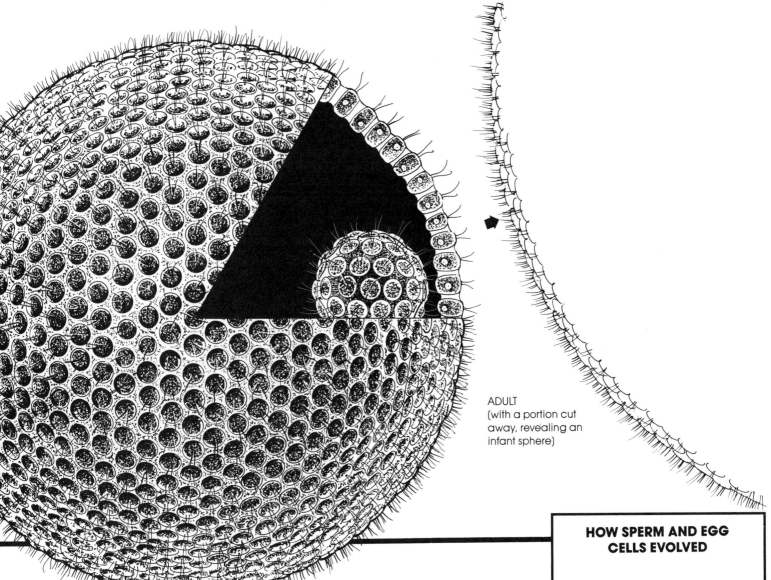

ADULT
(with a portion cut
away, revealing an
infant sphere)

no longer identical in appearance. One became larger and one smaller, yet both kept their tails. They alone were able to swim away from the sphere colony and start others.

In the largest colonies there were up to 50,000 cells. A few existed for reproduction only. It was at this stage that the gametes took on their identities as egg and sperm cells.

Eggs became larger and lost their tails. Sperm became smaller and enlarged their tails. Eggs grew larger,

holding more food for the developing embryo. Sperm became smaller and their tails pushed them even faster. Eggs waited on the surface of the sphere for the sperm to arrive. Sperm swam outside the sphere, struggling to reach the egg as quickly as possible or die trying.

Whether from sexual union or simple budding, new colonies grew protected within the sphere. The offspring escaped with a jelly-dissolving hormone that split a temporary seam in the parent sphere. This was the earliest form of "giving birth."

HOW SPERM AND EGG CELLS EVOLVED

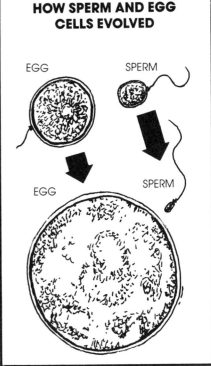

EGG

SPERM

EGG

SPERM

The Planula—fill 'er up!

The reproductive cells in a blastula (see page 22) get a free ride. They are fed by neighboring cells and take up valuable real estate on the surface. Reproductive cells are better off inside the sphere, where they are not only sheltered but also out of the way.

Sometimes other surface cells also enter the sphere along with the gametes. Shaped like wandering amoebas, they become special food digesters. The surface cells engulf prey and pass it unaltered to the inside, where these special cells eat it and distribute the digested nutrients among the other cells.

A planula forms when a sphere colony elongates and fills with digestive cells, reproductive cells, and gelatin. Planula means "little flat one." It is the larva, or immature form, of a hydra, a simple microscopic relative of corals and jellyfish.

Planulas have been described as the simplest, most primitive animals known. The ancestors of all animals, including jellyfish and their kin, must have resembled planulas.

Planulas have special sensory cells on one end. Sensory cells surround stingers in mature hydras and signal them when to fire. These sensory cells are the forerunners of animal nervous tissue. Nervous tissue sends messages to other parts of the body better than cytoplasm does.

Each surface cell of a planula produces one cell whip. Together all the whips sense prey and help the planula move about. The base of each surface cell extends and interconnects with its neighbors, acting like muscles between the cells. They contract and stretch out as the planula creeps or swims. The planula does not maintain a round shape as it moves. Parts of its body move forward and backward.

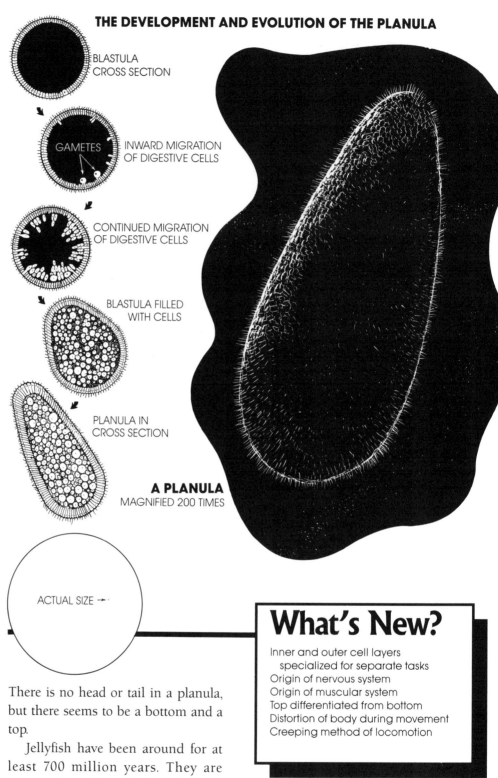

THE DEVELOPMENT AND EVOLUTION OF THE PLANULA

BLASTULA
CROSS SECTION

GAMETES

INWARD MIGRATION
OF DIGESTIVE CELLS

CONTINUED MIGRATION
OF DIGESTIVE CELLS

BLASTULA FILLED
WITH CELLS

PLANULA IN
CROSS SECTION

A PLANULA
MAGNIFIED 200 TIMES

ACTUAL SIZE →

There is no head or tail in a planula, but there seems to be a bottom and a top.

Jellyfish have been around for at least 700 million years. They are among the earliest fossils of multicelled animals known at present. Planulas, unknown in the fossil record, must have started out some 50 million years earlier.

What's New?

Inner and outer cell layers
    specialized for separate tasks
Origin of nervous system
Origin of muscular system
Top differentiated from bottom
Distortion of body during movement
Creeping method of locomotion

The Lost World of the Ediacara Animals

The 700-million-year-old jelly-fish previously mentioned may not have been a jellyfish after all but an organism with no living descendents. The earliest known fossils of animals large enough to have been seen by the naked eye come from a time known as the Ediacaran period, after the town in Australia in which their fossils were first reported. Since then, similar fossils have turned up all around the world.

Along with a number of worm burrows, Ediacaran fossils include many unusual flat, soft-bodied animals. Some radiate like spokes on a wheel. They look like flattened jellyfish remains. Others radiate like veins on a leaf along a central shaft. All of them are as flat as a pancake, and their many lobes seem to have been quilted together.

Planulas shifted their digestive cells to the inside. These organisms seem to have kept all of their cells on the surface, like giant deflated blastulas.

In that case, the quilting on their surfaces would have given their bodies extra strength to avoid being ripped apart by waves and tides.

Planulas survived while these animals did not. Why? We may never know.

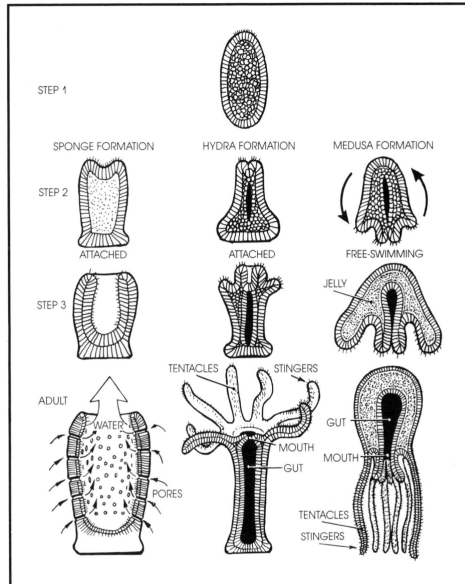

How a Planula Grows Up

A planula, or something very much like it, is the larval form of the simplest of all animals, the sponge, the hydra, and the jellyfish.

A sponge larva attaches itself to the seafloor and develops an infolding that assumes a cup shape. Tiny pores open in the sides of the cup, and cilia on the inside create a current through the pores.

A polyp, such as a hydra, grows in a similar fashion at first. But stinging, grasping tentacles soon grow from around the lip of its cup. No pores ever form on its sides.

A medusa, or jellyfish, can be thought of as an upside-down polyp that lives in open water.

The Simple Flatworm—get your tail moving, creep!

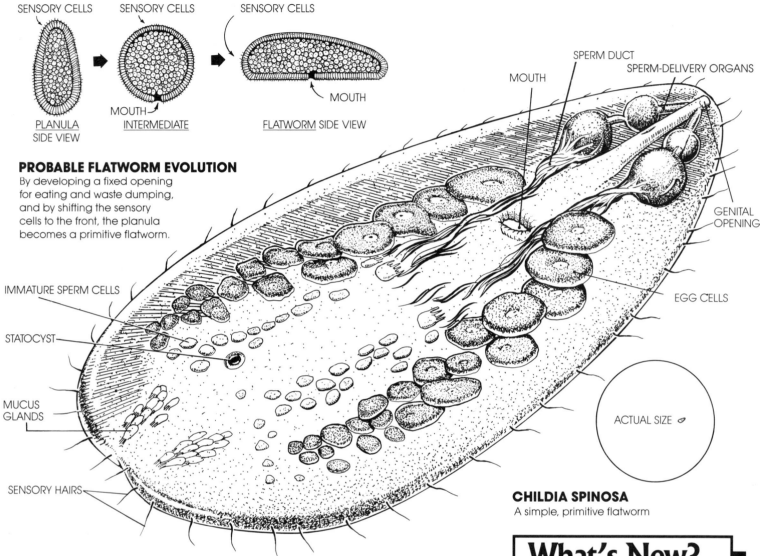

SENSORY CELLS | SENSORY CELLS | SENSORY CELLS

PLANULA SIDE VIEW — MOUTH INTERMEDIATE — MOUTH FLATWORM SIDE VIEW

PROBABLE FLATWORM EVOLUTION
By developing a fixed opening for eating and waste dumping, and by shifting the sensory cells to the front, the planula becomes a primitive flatworm.

SPERM DUCT
MOUTH
SPERM-DELIVERY ORGANS
GENITAL OPENING
EGG CELLS

IMMATURE SPERM CELLS
STATOCYST
MUCUS GLANDS
SENSORY HAIRS

ACTUAL SIZE

CHILDIA SPINOSA
A simple, primitive flatworm

What's New?

A fixed body opening (mouth/anus)
Genital opening
Left and right sides identical
Statocyst (organ of balance)
Sensory hairs
Cross-body muscles
Concentration of nerve net in the "head"
Reproductive cells near the tail

Instead of maturing into a spectacular swimming, stinging jellyfish, the poor, primitive flatworm remains tiny and flat, spending its life silently creeping about on the ocean floor.

The greatest advance of the flatworm was its developing a single fixed opening for both eating food and dumping solid waste. Always found near the center of the lower side, this opening is often called the mouth. It also functions as the anus and is usually located closer to the tail. As the simple flatworm has no stomach, this new opening is merely the gateway to the special digestive cells on the inside. The interesting thing is that not only does food go into this opening on its way to the digestive cells but sometimes the digestive cells pour out of this opening like applesauce to surround and digest food outside the body. They return only after dinner is finished. Simple flatworms eat other flatworms and other tiny animals. They also eat diatoms (one-celled sea plants) and any larger dead organism that may sink to the seafloor.

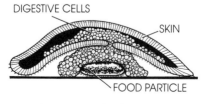

DIGESTIVE CELLS
SKIN
FOOD PARTICLE

HOW A FLATWORM EATS

Simple flatworms find their prey with special sensory cells clustered mostly at the front of their body. Sensory bristles may be present, but eyes are not.

Like most multi-celled animals, flatworms have a special organ called a statocyst that tells them when they are right side up. Flatworms creep over all sorts of seafloor obstacles. Sometimes they crawl up sheer cliffs. The statocyst (or "stationary sack") is a fluid-filled chamber with a tiny particle of lime inside. This particle sits on the tips of sensory "hairs" similar to cell whips. When the flatworm tilts to one side, the particle falls to that side, bending the sensory "hairs" in that direction, which signals the situation to the nervous system. In

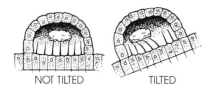

NOT TILTED   TILTED

HOW A STATOCYST WORKS

this way, flatworms maintain their sense of balance. In all fish and higher vertebrates, including humans, tilting is sensed with a pair of similar but reshaped organs, the semicircular canals of the inner ear (see page 40), located next to the sound sensors.

Most of a flatworm's nerves surround the statocyst. These nerves form the beginning of the brain.

Flatworms typically travel in one direction only. They are guided by the part of the body with the most sensory cells. Although not separated from the rest of the body, this leading edge is often called the head. Opposite the head is the tail.

Flatworms are bilateral ("two-sided") animals because, like a human, their left and right sides are mirror images of each other. Because of their flat shape, flatworms also have a definite topside and bottom.

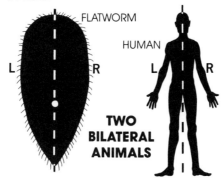

FLATWORM
HUMAN
L   R   L   R

TWO BILATERAL ANIMALS

Minute flatworms swim within bottom debris. Larger species creep about on the surface. Cilia push the flatworm along as if it were riding on a thousand pairs of stilts. A flatworm's flattened shape means that a greater surface area is in contact with whatever it is creeping on. Subsurface muscles are used to turn and twist the body. These muscles crisscross the entire body between the upper and lower skin layers and are as transparent as the skin is. Muscle power becomes increasingly important the larger the flatworm becomes.

Gland cells form in the skin layer or just beneath it. Some provide mucus or slime on which the flatworm creeps, like a snail. Other glands provide glue to help keep a flatworm stuck to a rock where waves might otherwise knock it off. Still other glands produce a substance that breaks down the glue so that the flatworm can move on.

Those flatworms that live in beach sand where the spaces between the sand grains are not continually filled with water are the most specialized. They usually have longer, more worm-like bodies for moving between grains of sand.

A large portion of the flatworm's body is devoted to producing both sperm and egg cells. When two flatworms meet, they fertilize each other with small extendable tubes for conducting sperm. The fertilized eggs are released in one of three ways: by passing through the mouth/anus, by passing through a genital opening near the tail, or by rupturing through a weak spot somewhere in the surface layer of cells. The best way to handle the laying of eggs had not yet become standardized.

Most flatworms are unusual among animals in that their sperm cells have two tails and these tails have a 9-plus-0 microtubule organization. At least one species, however, does have a conventional sperm tail.

Some flatworms produce eggs with a yolk, the way most animals do. Others produce separate yolk cells that envelope fertilized yolkless eggs while they are being deposited.

Despite the fact that flatworms have so much of their bodies devoted to producing egg and sperm cells, many reproduce by simply dividing in two. They are not the most advanced animals capable of reproducing without sex. Some lizards and beetles are known to bear young without the need of a mate.

Today, flatworms are common in temperate and arctic seas. They are bottom dwellers that are typically found under rocks, among algae, and on mud. The lifespan of a flatworm may be from 1 to 5 months long.

Flatworms are unknown in the fossil record, but that should come as no surprise. They are mostly made up of water and are so small that fossils would be hard to identify. They probably originated 850 million years ago.

The Advanced Flatworm—guts, brains, and more!

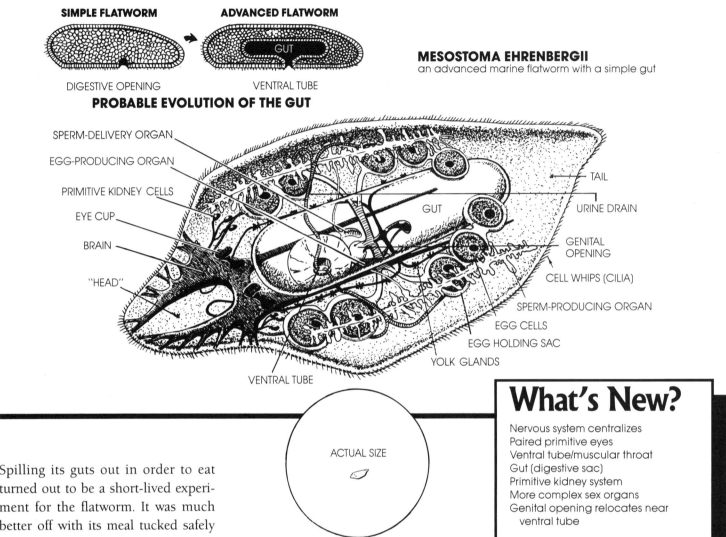

SIMPLE FLATWORM   **ADVANCED FLATWORM**

GUT

DIGESTIVE OPENING   VENTRAL TUBE

PROBABLE EVOLUTION OF THE GUT

MESOSTOMA EHRENBERGII
an advanced marine flatworm with a simple gut

SPERM-DELIVERY ORGAN

EGG-PRODUCING ORGAN

PRIMITIVE KIDNEY CELLS

EYE CUP

BRAIN

"HEAD"

GUT

TAIL

URINE DRAIN

GENITAL OPENING

CELL WHIPS (CILIA)

SPERM-PRODUCING ORGAN

EGG CELLS

EGG HOLDING SAC

YOLK GLANDS

VENTRAL TUBE

ACTUAL SIZE

What's New?

Nervous system centralizes
Paired primitive eyes
Ventral tube/muscular throat
Gut (digestive sac)
Primitive kidney system
More complex sex organs
Genital opening relocates near
   ventral tube

Spilling its guts out in order to eat turned out to be a short-lived experiment for the flatworm. It was much better off with its meal tucked safely inside during digestion. The organ that makes this possible is the gut, digestive cells which form an empty sack that functions as both a stomach and intestine.

A gut is one of the first things that the embryos of all higher animals develop. One side of the blastula (see pages 22-23) develops a dimple that continues to get deeper and deeper. Imagine poking an inflated balloon with your finger until one side touches the other. In the same way, a portion of the outside cell layer becomes an inside layer with a new function—digestion.

In some flatworms, the gut is a simple sac. In others, it branches off into hundreds of tiny sacs. Connecting the gut to the flatworm's mouth/anus opening is the ventral tube. The pharynx (or "throat") is a muscular portion of this tube that can protrude outside the flatworm, like a vacuum cleaner hose, to grasp prey.

In simple flatworms, the nervous system is a loose weave of nerve cells. In advanced flatworms, it becomes a separate, easily visible set of tissues. This central nervous system is made up of a pair of nerve cords. They run along both sides of the gut to the "head," where they form something like a brain. Many branching filaments also lead from the "brain" to the sensory cells.

Above the brain are two eyes. In their most primitive form, eyes are essentially highly modified nerve endings shaped like cups and surrounded by pigment cells. They cannot focus images but can sense light and from which direction it comes. Many flatworms try to avoid light.

One of the important activities of every cell in microscopic animals is waste excretion. Waste is made up primarily of water and salt. As the

The Last Billion Years of Animals

The major living phyla, or primary divisions of the animal kingdom according to body type, are diagrammed at the right. Their most likely relationships to one another are also shown. By the Cambrian period, nearly all the major living phyla had appeared. Unfamiliar labels on this chart are explained in upcoming pages (see Index).

number of cells in an animal rises, this activity is turned over to specialized cells, cells that perform only this function. In advanced flatworms, primitive kidney cells filter cell fluids for wastes. Urine collects in tiny tubes that drain out the ventral tube.

In advanced flatworms, the sperm- and egg-producing organs become more complex. The genital opening moves to just behind the ventral tube.

All told, flatworms can reproduce in four different ways: by producing gametes (sex cells), by fission (splitting in two), by budding off little flatworms, or by regenerating lost parts. A flatworm chopped into 10 equal pieces can become 10 fully functional flatworms.

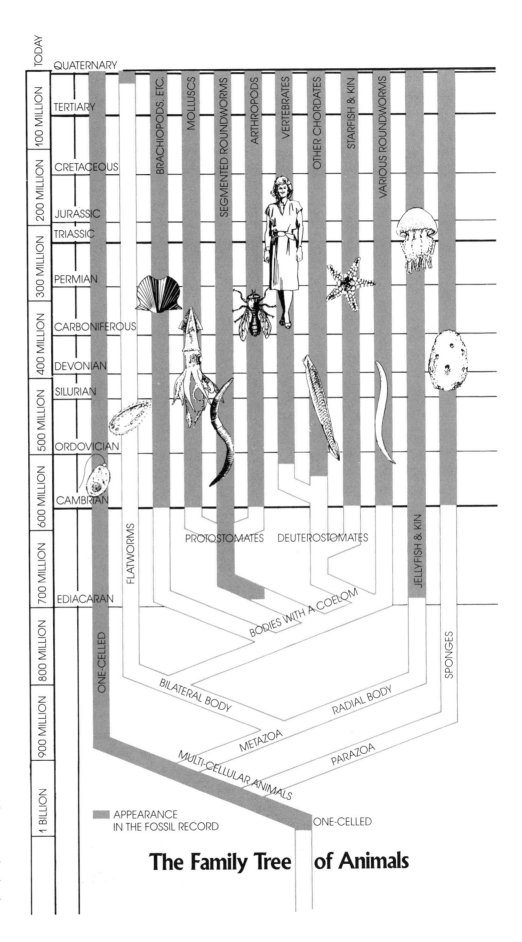

The Family Tree of Animals

The Ribbon Worm—food in one end and out the other.

Flatworms have only one digestive opening, and so they run the risk of mixing incoming food and outgoing waste. Nemertines, or ribbon worms, are the most primitive animals that have solved this problem. They have a mouth in front that moves forward to seize food, and an anus in the rear that moves away from expelled waste. The mouth and the anus are connected by an intestine. A layer of skin and muscle cells closely wraps this one-way tube.

How ribbon worms evolved from flatworms is not clear. There are some living species that provide important clues.

There is a living flatworm with both a ventral tube and an additional sucker located beneath its "head." This sucker is formed from an infolding of surface cells. It is as if someone had poked a finger gently into an inflated balloon to produce this skin depression. The sucker does not connect to the wall of the gut, but if it did, a complete mouth/intestine/anus system would have developed, as exists in ribbon worms. The mouth of a human embryo also appears in just this way, on the outer cell wall far from the original gut opening.

Ribbon worms are suckers. They suck in fish and other worms, like kids suck in spaghetti. Early jawless fish also took in food in this way.

Like flatworms, ribbon worms have flattened or rounded bodies covered with cell whips, or cilia. They use cilia to creep over a trail of excreted slime. Inside the intestine, cell whips keep food moving from one end to the other.

Ribbon worm muscle fibers are arranged like the basket weaving of "Chinese handcuffs," a toy children use to snare their fingers in. To move, ribbon worms bunch up and stretch

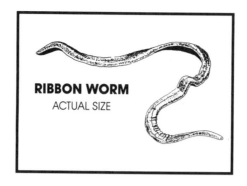

RIBBON WORM
ACTUAL SIZE

What's New?

Mouth in front, anus in rear, with a linear intestine connecting the two
Circulatory system/blood
Individuals separated into sexes
Sucking method of eating
Nerves centralized to head
Basket-weave muscular system
Active at night

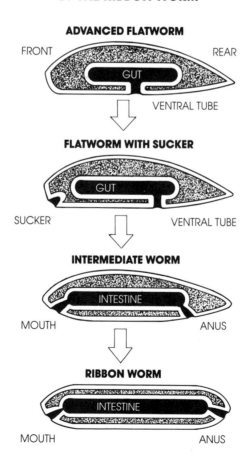

THE PROBABLE EVOLUTION OF THE RIBBON WORM

ADVANCED FLATWORM
FRONT   REAR
GUT
VENTRAL TUBE

FLATWORM WITH SUCKER
GUT
SUCKER   VENTRAL TUBE

INTERMEDIATE WORM
INTESTINE
MOUTH   ANUS

RIBBON WORM
INTESTINE
MOUTH   ANUS

out. Species that swim do so with eel-like motions.

Typically 1 to 8 inches long, ribbon worms are larger than typical marine flatworms. Their inner tissues are farther from the surface. Therefore, these tissues need to be fed nutrients and oxygen by blood. A ribbon worm's simple circulatory system is so primitive that there may be as few as two blood vessels, one on either side of the intestine. They are connected to one another near the mouth and near the anus. The flow of blood is very irregular. It may depend on the contractions of the blood vessels themselves or upon the overall contractions of the worm itself. Often the blood is clear. Sometimes, however, it contains corpuscles that may be red (like human blood corpuscles), orange, green, or yellow. White blood cells, which attack invading organisms, are also present.

In ribbon worms, the nerves are more concentrated in the snout than they are in flatworms. Two to 6 eyes are often there as well. Ribbon worms use their eyes to avoid light; they are active only at night.

Ribbon worms are the most primitive animals in which the sexes are separated into only male and only female individuals. Males produce sperm only. Females produce eggs only. Not any ribbon worm will do for a mate; one of the opposite sex must be found.

Living ribbon worms have certain features that remove them from human ancestry (see chart on facing page). Nevertheless, something very much like a ribbon worm, with the features described in this text, was a human ancestor. Fossils of ribbon worms are known from the middle Cambrian period, 530 million years ago.

The Roundworm—it "swims" through the sand.

Primitive roundworms, or nematodes, are colorless, unsegmented, tough little predators. Their body is usually cylinder-shaped and tapered at both ends. In these respects they resemble hatchling fish. A roundworm has no outer cilia on which to creep, so like a fish, it moves its entire body to make snaky S-curves between the grains of sand or dirt in which it lives.

Roundworms have no cilia inside their bodies, either. Even their sperm have no tails. Chordate ancestors were probably roundworms that did not lose their inner cilia and sperm tails.

Roundworms have something close to a coelom, or body cavity. It is a space within a layer of cells between the intestine and the skin where new organs develop. The appearance of the first true coelom is discussed on page 32.

Within the roundworm's false coelom, its organs float freely in a jellylike fluid. This fluid is under pressure

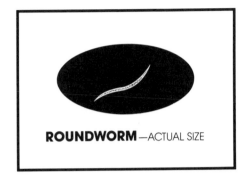

ROUNDWORM—ACTUAL SIZE

What's New?

Hydrostatic skeleton/stiffened body
Loss of external cilia
Undulating method of burrowing
Tough skin
Tapered shape

beneath the roundworm's tough outer skin. The pressure acts like water in a fire hose to stiffen the worm along its entire length. Such body support created by liquid under pressure is called a hydrostatic skeleton ("fluid-

at-rest skeleton"). This type of skeleton was an important forerunner to one made of bone.

Fossil roundworms are known from the Carboniferous period, 300 million years ago, but some of the earliest worm fossils are 700-million-year-old burrows, tiny winding tunnels in the seafloor. It takes a tough animal to burrow through sand or mud, and no animal then had hard parts, such as a shell or a bony skeleton. Worms with a coelom and a tough hydrostatic skeleton must have created those burrows.

Roundworms eat organic debris and live prey, but many living today have become parasites. Pork should never be eaten raw because of the threat of roundworm infection. The roundworm population greatly outnumbers that of all other kinds of animals. They can be found in great numbers in the soil, fresh water, and seabeds.

DEUTEROSTOMATES & PROTOSTOMATES

Animals with both a mouth and an anus can be divided according to the way their embryo develops, among other criteria.

In protostomates ("first mouth") such as segmented worms and their kin, the first opening that appears in their blastula ultimately becomes a mouth. In deuterostomates ("secondary mouth") that same opening ultimately becomes an anus. Humans and

starfish and their kin develop in this way. Bryozoans and brachiopods are sea creatures with similarities to both groups.

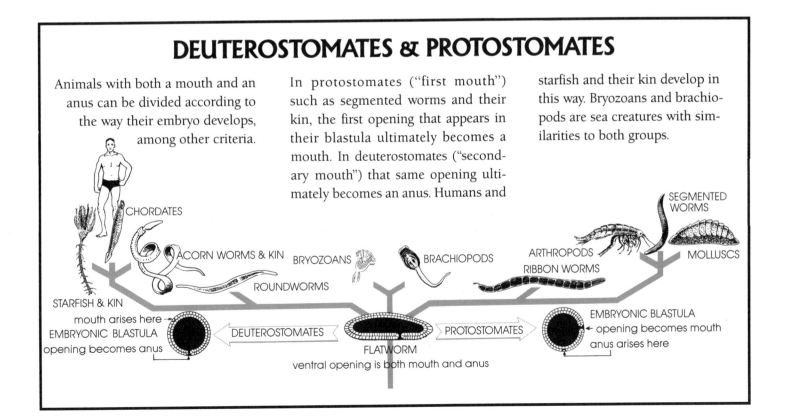

CHORDATES
ACORN WORMS & KIN
BRYOZOANS
BRACHIOPODS
SEGMENTED WORMS
ARTHROPODS
RIBBON WORMS
MOLLUSCS
ROUNDWORMS
STARFISH & KIN
mouth arises here
EMBRYONIC BLASTULA
opening becomes anus
DEUTEROSTOMATES
PROTOSTOMATES
EMBRYONIC BLASTULA
opening becomes mouth
anus arises here
FLATWORM
ventral opening is both mouth and anus

The Wormlike Chordate—a stiff back was a big advantage.

It is easy to see that an earthworm's body is divided into dozens of short segments. Each segment is separated from its neighboring ones by thin muscular walls. With more muscles to the inch, segmented worms have more control over their body movements than unsegmented worms do.

Human ancestors went through a segmented worm stage. Earthworms, however, were not a part of human ancestry. They are related to squids and horseflies. Unfortunately, no worms are known, either in the fossil record or alive today, that come close to being a model ancestor for this stage of human evolution. Scientists have guessed what this missing link must have looked like and how it came to be. This wormlike segmented ancestor would have evolved some 650 million to 600 million years ago, and it would have had a true coelom.

As touched on earlier, a coelom is an important space that develops between the intestinal tube and the skin. A tough hydrostatic skeleton results from the pressure of fluids within the coelom. This space provides an opportunity for other important organs to develop. All animals more complex than worms have a coelom. The coelom develops one way in all protostomates and another way in all deuterostomates (see page 31).

In our ancestors, the way the coelom probably came to be is described and illustrated in the following four steps:

1. Beginning with the ancestral roundworm, the intestine was a straight tube that ran from mouth to anus.

2. Later, a series of pockets, like little stomachs, developed along the length of this tube. These little stomachs provided pit stops for food and

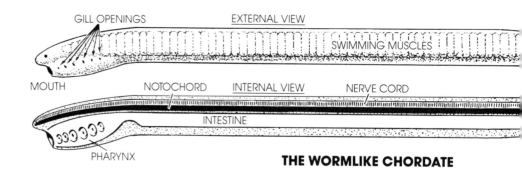

THE WORMLIKE CHORDATE

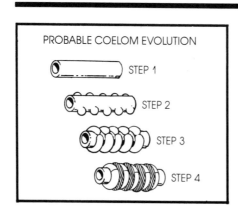

PROBABLE COELOM EVOLUTION

STEP 1

STEP 2

STEP 3

STEP 4

What's New?

Notochord
Spinal cord
Segmented coelom
Banded swimming muscles
Gill openings
Coordinated swimming primarily
  with lateral undulations

digestive juices. At first they simply improved digestion. But being attached to the skin as well, they also had an effect on the worm's performance whenever it tried to move. Those worms that could match the filling and emptying of their intestinal pockets with the action of their skin muscles helped themselves move better.

3. As time went by, these little stomachs grew larger and larger. Finally they formed a series of paired half rings along the entire length of the tubular intestine. At this stage the worm probably looked like a tiny pack of roll candy.

4. Over, around, and between each ring segment, thin sheets of muscles developed. They squeezed the contents of the ring segments into the intestine and let them fill back up again.

Over time, this series of ring segments and muscles proved to be more useful in moving the worm from place to place than in helping it to digest food. When the last tiny opening between each ring segment and the intestine finally became sealed off, coelom segments were created.

From that time forward, the ring segments acted more like sealed water balloons. Whenever they were squeezed in one direction, they popped out in the other, usually against a neighboring ring segment. At this point our ancestor had a segmented hydrostatic skeleton, much like that of an earthworm.

An earthworm can move in three ways: (1) It can undulate from side to side like a snake. (2) It can telescope; that is, stretch out its front then pull up its rear. (3) It can move by peristalsis; in other words, segments expand in a wave to push the worm along. In humans, food is pushed all the way

This is what a wormlike chordate might have looked like. This drawing is based on a roundworm and a primitive chordate, the lancelet (see page 34). The wormlike chordate was probably both a burrowing and a swimming animal feeding on single-celled organisms on the seafloor 650 million years ago.

EARLY CHORDATE
PROBABLE
ACTUAL SIZE

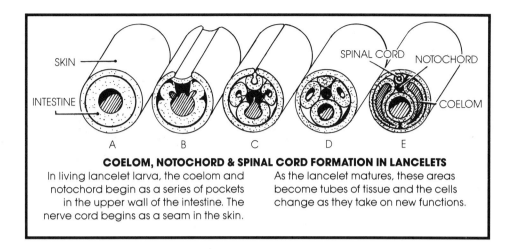

SKIN

INTESTINE

SPINAL CORD   NOTOCHORD

COELOM

A   B   C   D   E

COELOM, NOTOCHORD & SPINAL CORD FORMATION IN LANCELETS

In living lancelet larva, the coelom and notochord begin as a series of pockets in the upper wall of the intestine. The nerve cord begins as a seam in the skin.

As the lancelet matures, these areas become tubes of tissue and the cells change as they take on new functions.

through the digestive system by peristalsis.

We can see from the activities of earthworms that undulating, telescoping, and peristalsis are perfect for burrowing and creeping in soil, but telescoping and peristalsis are not well suited for swimming in open water. In order to swim well, a segmented worm needs to stiffen its body so that it won't telescope whenever the swimming muscles contract.

The organ that stiffened our segmented worm ancestor was a notochord. It is a firm yet flexible rod that prevented telescoping and peristalsis. Lancelets and some fish still have a notochord. These animals don't bunch up and stretch out. They undulate from side to side.

As the muscles on either side of the notochord take turns contracting, they bend the notochord to the left and to the right. When the muscles relax, the notochord springs back like a diving board, which is one way this elastic rod saves energy.

The notochord first formed from the top of the intestine along its entire length.

All animals with a notochord are chordates. A human embryo also develops a notochord, but shortly thereafter it is replaced with a backbone.

After the notochord appeared, the coelom segments became useless and dwindled away, leaving a simple large coelom space. In their place, the coelom-squeezing muscles continued to grow and develop into powerful swimming muscles. Lancelets (see page 34) and fish have huge muscles, which make them good to eat.

With muscle blocks contracting rhythmically on either side of its body, a chordate (such as a fish) swims with graceful side-to-side undulations. Coordinating this rhythm is the job of the central nerve cord in the back above the notochord. Where did it come from?

As seen earlier, advanced flatworms have a pair of nerve cords along either side of their gut. A roundworm is similar but also has smaller cords running down its belly and back. In chordates, a nerve cord formed in the back, close to the notochord and the swimming muscles attached to the notochord.

By swimming from place to place, rather than burrowing, chordates could get to more feeding sites more quickly. They could also escape bottom-dwelling predators. Better swimmers kept evolving. Those with larger, flatter tails were better at pushing back more water with every undulation. The streamlined shape that evolved created a minimum of drag. Long, low fins provided stability in water. Like feathers on an arrow, they kept the chordate pointing straight and sure toward its destination.

An early wormlike chordate would have fed on single-celled organisms that drifted along the shallow seafloor. It would have spent its days sucking in and spitting out food and water. At least some of the food would have stuck to the inside of its throat. A coat of mucus made the throat sticky. Cilia (cell whips) continually swept food particles back toward the intestine.

After millions of years, the chordate developed side exits, called gill openings, to flush out the excess water it was sucking in. This one-way pump proved to be a much better way to trap food particles.

Although today most fish breathe with gills, at this early stage gills were not present. There were only gill openings. Oxygen was still being absorbed directly through the naked scaleless skin of the chordate.

The Lancelet—it swims by night and burrows by day.

The lancelet is a swimming animal sometimes known as the "headless fish." Among living animals, it most closely resembles the ancestor of all chordates. Fossil lancelets go back as far as 530 million years ago. Although they are built for swimming, living lancelets survive by avoiding daylight predators, such as fish, which evolved later. During the day, lancelets burrow, something human ancestors never went back to once they had begun swimming.

Lancelets swim by night to areas that are dense with plankton (microscopic sea life). Large numbers of adults gather together and bury themselves tail first in sand or gravel. Feathery mouth parts permit only plankton and water into their mouths, keeping sand out. Microscopic food is trapped on mucus strands, while excess water is flushed out the many dozen gill openings.

The lancelet swims like a fish, with rapid side-to-side flicks of its entire body. On the top, the lancelet has a low dorsal fin. On the bottom, there is a low ventral fin. These fins merge at the tail to form a caudal fin. These increase the lancelet's surface area to push water backward. They are supported and shaped by fin rays. This hardened tissue is the forerunner of an internal skeleton made of bone.

Near the lancelet's snout, on either side of the nerve cord, are two small spots that may be sensitive to light. A nerve also leads to a small pit in the snout that may be a smelling organ. Evidently neither is very important. With its stationary mode of feeding, the lancelet has little need for eyes and a nose.

Digestion takes place in the lancelet partly as it does in the planula and flatworm, by roving digestive cells

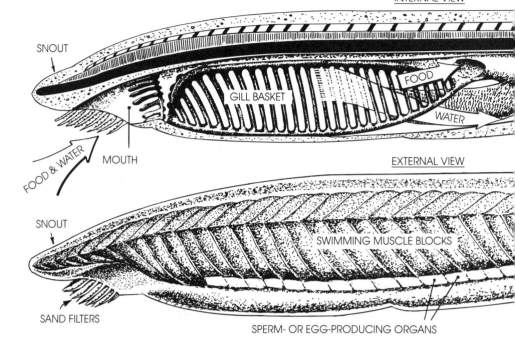

THE YOUNG LANCELET

INTERNAL VIEW

SNOUT

GILL BASKET

FOOD

WATER

FOOD & WATER

MOUTH

EXTERNAL VIEW

SNOUT

SWIMMING MUSCLE BLOCKS

SAND FILTERS

SPERM- OR EGG-PRODUCING ORGANS

What's New?

Swimming mode of locomotion
Dorsal, ventral, and caudal fins
supported by hard tissue
Larger tail muscles shift anus forward
Digestive juices
Thyroid and pituitary tissue
Arteries/veins
Larger size
External fertilization

PIKAIA
THE EARLIEST KNOWN CHORDATE
530 MILLION YEARS OLD
ACTUAL SIZE

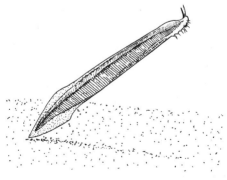

(pages 24 and 26). Secreted juices also play a part in digestion.

The tail of a lancelet is made up of large tail muscles and hard fin tissue. The anus lies forward of the tail tip, toward the left side of the lower tail fin.

The pale pink lancelet has no heart or red blood cells. Its colorless blood is pumped by contractions of large arteries and veins.

Special tissues in its throat are early pituitary and thyroid glands. Glands release chemicals the body finds useful. In humans, the pituitary gland stimulates growth and also stimulates other glands. The thyroid gland stimulates the rate at which the body burns energy and regulates the

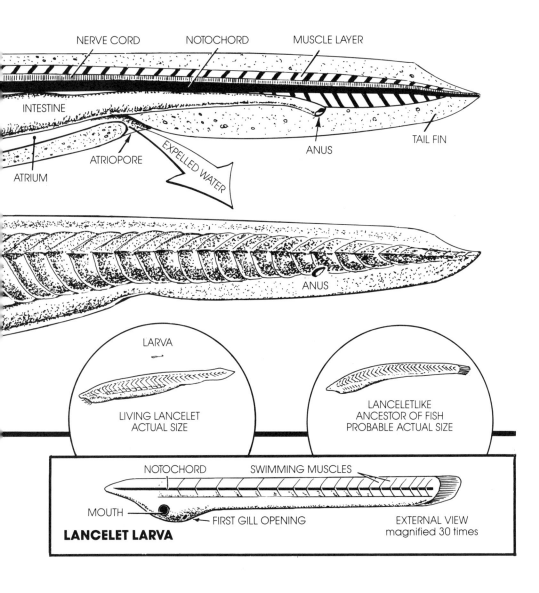

NERVE CORD   NOTOCHORD   MUSCLE LAYER

INTESTINE

ATRIOPORE
EXPELLED WATER

ATRIUM

ANUS

TAIL FIN

ANUS

LARVA

LIVING LANCELET
ACTUAL SIZE

LANCELETLIKE
ANCESTOR OF FISH
PROBABLE ACTUAL SIZE

NOTOCHORD   SWIMMING MUSCLES

MOUTH

FIRST GILL OPENING

EXTERNAL VIEW
magnified 30 times

LANCELET LARVA

THE SINUOUS
PATH OF A
SWIMMING
LANCELET
AS SEEN
FROM ABOVE

amount of calcium in the blood.

Lancelet females lay dozens of eggs in the water, where they are fertilized by the male's sperm. The male has no need of a special tube for conducting his sperm to the inside of the female. Therefore the lancelet, like most fish and amphibians, does not have a penis.

Hatchling lancelets probably look like their ancestors, the earliest chordates. They have a mouth and one gill opening for feeding. The larva swims at first along the bottom and later in the open water with the plankton.

As it matures, the living lancelet grows more gill openings until it has 100 or so. The lancelet ancestors of fish, in contrast, probably never grew more than 7 pairs of gill openings.

To protect its many tiny gill openings from clogging while burrowing, the living lancelet blankets them with folds of skin and muscle that enclose the gill openings within the body. Filtered waste water fills a space (the atrium) beneath these folds and is flushed out a rear opening (the atriopore) at regular intervals.

In contrast to living lancelets, the

lanceletlike ancestors of fish never returned to burrowing after first adopting a swimming life-style. A blanket for the gill openings, an atrium, and feathery sand filters are later developments fish ancestors never had.

As passive feeders, living lancelets need the cilia inside their throat to beat a current of water and plankton through their gill openings. As active hunters, the lanceletlike ancestors of fish kept swimming to keep a current of water and plankton flowing through their gill openings.

Chordates—the first 300 million years.

The chart to the right is an overview of the earliest chordates. One can easily trace the lineage of human ancestry by always staying to the right. Each left turn follows a different evolutionary path. Major advancements are noted along the way. Gray bars represent the known fossil record.

Chordates are animals stiffened by a notochord. In later chordates, known as vertebrates, segmented bone or cartilage replaces the notochord. The notochord was an important feature in the back of every fish and amphibian covered by this chart. In some cases it was ringed by bone or cartilage for greater strength. Today most fish and four-legged creatures have a notochord only as an embryo.

A chordate feeds with an open mouth while propelled forward through open water by a muscular, undulating body and tail. On land, legs propel a chordate forward.

Now let's take a look at the chart. Notice how only a small portion of human ancestry is actually known from fossils. Much of what we know about this period comes from looking at the level of advancement achieved by distant relatives in other branches of the chordate family tree.

Young sea squirts have a notochord and swim freely, but as adults they undergo a change. They become attached to the seafloor and filter feed much like a lancelet. Acorn worms, pterobranchs, sea lilies, and starfish are distantly related forms.

Except for lancelets and sea squirts, all chordates are craniates. Craniates have a cranium, or head. They also have eyes, nostrils, balancing organs, and a brain.

Conodonts are the earliest known craniates. They looked like living hagfish but had strange "teeth" lining their throats that may have been plankton filters.

Jawless fish had the first bony external skeleton. Early types ate plankton. Living lampreys are parasites of other fish.

Gnathostomes had the first jaws and paired fins. Their origin has not yet been documented in the fossil record.

Placoderms, named for their heavily armored "plate skins," were not closely related to other fish with jaws. Spiny sharks were related but had a single large spine supporting each fin. Both groups became extinct long ago.

Fish with fins made of many bony or cartilage filaments include most living fish. Cartilage is the flexible white support material that caps the ends of chicken bones. Sharks and ratfish have skeletons made of cartilage and flexible skins covered with tiny toothlike scales.

Primitive bony fish were covered with interlocking diamond-shaped scales made of bone. Many had bony internal skeletons as well.

Ray-finned fish had fin muscles inside the body wall, while lobe-fins had muscles extending into the fin itself. Among lobe-fins, only lungfish and the coelacanth survive to this day. The extinct rhipidistians had sharp teeth, strong skeletons, and broad lobes. Some rhipidistians, the panderichthyids, were the ancestors of amphibians.

As adults, amphibians had legs, but they hatched underwater with gills and fins. Ichthyostegids were the first known amphibians and gephyrostegids were the ones closest to reptiles.

Reptiles laid the first egg provided with a large yolk and a special watertight membrane.

Geologists tell us that during the Cambrian period, North America straddled the equator and was submerged beneath shallow seas. Only the area surrounding Hudson Bay from Greenland to Minnesota was low-lying land.

By the Ordovician period, even this area had become submerged. A new mountain range with many volcanoes emerged along the East Coast.

The Silurian was a peaceful period that saw the erosion of that eastern mountain chain into a series of islands. There was an uplifting of land along the east coast of Greenland.

North America was still flooded by the late Devonian period, but land in east Greenland provided a foothold for the first amphibians, insects, and land plants.

During the early Carboniferous period, a vast stretch of swampy lowlands appeared from the northern Canadian islands to Virginia. The forests that sprang up there were the home of giant insects and the first reptiles.

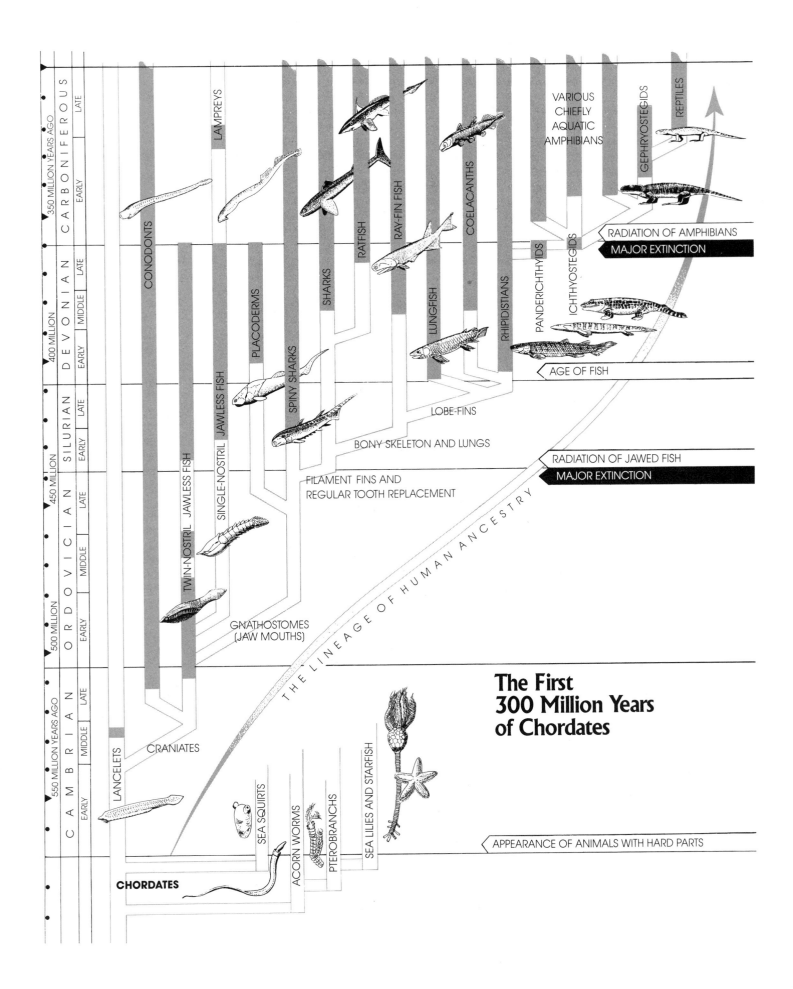

**The First
300 Million Years
of Chordates**

CAMBRIAN | ORDOVICIAN | SILURIAN | DEVONIAN | CARBONIFEROUS

550 MILLION YEARS AGO | 500 MILLION | 450 MILLION | 400 MILLION | 350 MILLION YEARS AGO

EARLY | MIDDLE | LATE | EARLY | MIDDLE | LATE | EARLY | LATE | EARLY | MIDDLE | LATE | EARLY | LATE

THE LINEAGE OF HUMAN ANCESTRY

CHORDATES

SEA SQUIRTS

ACORN WORMS

PTEROBRANCHS

SEA LILIES AND STARFISH

APPEARANCE OF ANIMALS WITH HARD PARTS

LANCELETS

CRANIATES

GNATHOSTOMES
(JAW MOUTHS)

TWIN-NOSTRIL JAWLESS FISH

SINGLE-NOSTRIL JAWLESS FISH

CONODONTS

LAMPREYS

PLACODERMS

SPINY SHARKS

FILAMENT FINS AND
REGULAR TOOTH REPLACEMENT

RADIATION OF JAWED FISH
MAJOR EXTINCTION

SHARKS

RATFISH

RAY-FIN FISH

BONY SKELETON AND LUNGS

LOBE-FINS

LUNGFISH

COELACANTHS

RHIPIDISTIANS

PANDERICHTHYIDS

ICHTHYOSTEGIDS

AGE OF FISH

VARIOUS
CHIEFLY
AQUATIC
AMPHIBIANS

GEPHYROSTEGIDS

REPTILES

RADIATION OF AMPHIBIANS
MAJOR EXTINCTION

The First Fish—it pushed a head with its tail and ahead with

Fish are lancelet relatives that never adopted a burrowing life-style. They swam in pursuit of their prey. Resembling modern tadpoles, these early fish wriggled their tails to propel themselves from one feeding station to another. They had neither jaws nor stabilizing fins.

Fish have a more active life-style and burn energy at a higher rate than lower chordates do. Their bodies need more food, burn more oxygen, and produce more waste. Fish have a more muscular body and tail and a muscular mouth for pursuing and capturing food. Red blood, which can carry more oxygen than clear blood, is pumped to the cells by a muscular heart. Gills appear near the gill openings to provide the body with more oxygen, especially during a chase.

In lancelets, swimming muscles extend to the tip of the snout. In contrast, fish have only a few muscles on their head. The main ones that remain are those that move the eyeballs and the flexible throat. The head of a fish is like the radar system of a guided missile. It tastes, smells, sees, and then decides the best place to go to feed the mouth. The job of the trunk and the tail is to push the head where it wants to go.

Fish have increasingly complex sense organs. Most, but not all, are located in the head.

Three eyes appear on early fish, one on each side of the head, one on top. The top eye probably never formed a clear image as did the lateral, or side, eyes. Instead, it acted more like a light-sensitive gland. It gauged daily and seasonal changes in sunlight and released body chemicals at the correct time to stimulate egg and sperm production. Today, this gland is known as the pineal, and it is usually

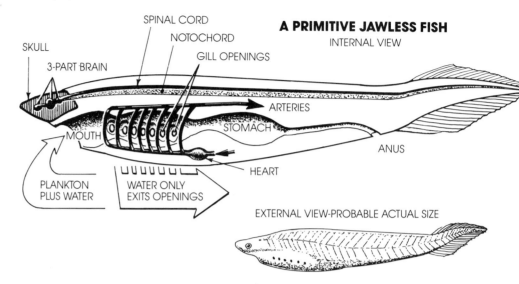

A PRIMITIVE JAWLESS FISH
INTERNAL VIEW

SKULL
3-PART BRAIN
SPINAL CORD
NOTOCHORD
GILL OPENINGS
ARTERIES
STOMACH
ANUS
MOUTH
HEART
PLANKTON PLUS WATER
WATER ONLY EXITS OPENINGS

EXTERNAL VIEW-PROBABLE ACTUAL SIZE

AN EARLY JAWLESS FISH

Unknown either as a living animal or as a fossil, this fish has a design based on the lancelet and a number of jawless fish. It would have lived during the middle Cambrian period, 530 million years ago.

What's New?

Head with braincase
Three-part brain
Eyes with lenses
Third eye
Nostrils
Semicircular canals
Electrosensory organs
Lateral-line organs
Higher rate of metabolism
Larger tail with upward bend
Heart and red blood
Kidneys
Stomach
Liver
Cloaca (see page 41)
Gills

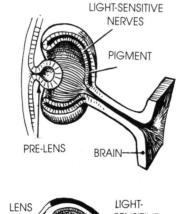

THE DEVELOPMENT OF THE EYE

LIGHT-SENSITIVE NERVES
PIGMENT
PRE-LENS
BRAIN

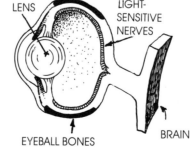

LENS
LIGHT-SENSITIVE NERVES
EYEBALL BONES
BRAIN

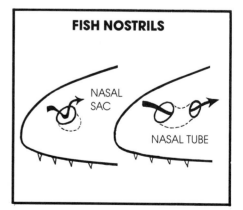

FISH NOSTRILS

NASAL SAC
NASAL TUBE

ts brain.

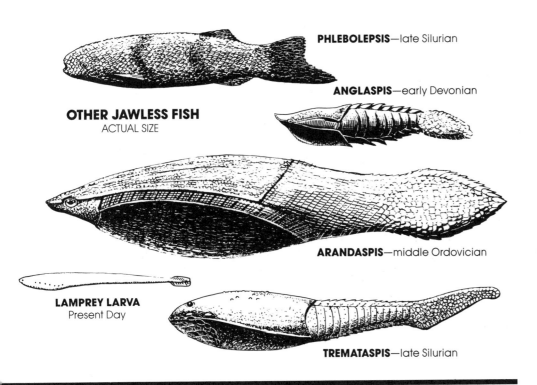

PHLEBOLEPSIS—late Silurian

ANGLASPIS—early Devonian

OTHER JAWLESS FISH
ACTUAL SIZE

ARANDASPIS—middle Ordovician

LAMPREY LARVA
Present Day

TREMATASPIS—late Silurian

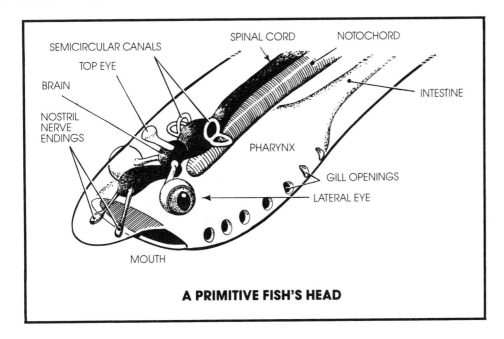

SEMICIRCULAR CANALS SPINAL CORD NOTOCHORD

TOP EYE

BRAIN

NOSTRIL
NERVE
ENDINGS

INTESTINE

PHARYNX

GILL OPENINGS

LATERAL EYE

MOUTH

A PRIMITIVE FISH'S HEAD

The semicircular canals were elaborate balancing organs on either side of the head to the rear of the eyes. They were made up of one or two loops of tissue filled with fluids and several hard, free-moving ear stones. These acted like the statocysts in flatworms (see page 27). Whenever the fish swam in other than an upright position, these ear stones moved over sensitive nerve endings in the loops. This signaled the situation to the brain, and the fish could right itself.

The most primitive fish had paired nostrils. These were small sacs in the skin connected to nerve endings. They sampled trace molecules of whatever was about to enter the mouth.

With odor signals, vision signals, and balance signals all coming in at once, the nervous system needed help. Three areas in the front part of the spinal chord became larger and specialized for smell, sight, and coordination. Together they formed the brain.

A braincase of cartilage developed. It protected the brain from injury and also provided strong tissues for the fragile sensory organs to nest in.

Driving the mouth and the sense organs toward food was the powerful body and tail. As the tail muscles enlarged, the rear part of the intestine and its opening, the anus, continued shifting forward. The anus stopped just behind the genital opening (where it remains in humans). It really didn't matter where the waste dump opening was, but the tail had to push from behind.

Our earliest fragmentary records of jawless fish come from the late Cambrian period. More complete jawless fish of various kinds, some of which are illustrated above, appear in later periods. Not one has been shown to be ancestral to jawed fishes, however.

buried deep within the brain, as it is in humans.

A fish's lateral eyes are provided with a lens to focus light on the sensitive tissues at the back of the eyeball to form an image. As free-swimming animals, fish need to see where they are going, what they are hunting, and where their enemies are. At first, only black-and-white vision was available. Gradually bony fish did see some color. Sharks never did.

Bones, Scales, Gills, and Guts.

We take for granted that a fish has its bony skeleton on the inside. It wasn't always that way. About 100 million years before bone appeared on the inside, some early fish had a skeleton made of bone on the outside. In addition to bone, this external skeleton had layers of the materials found in present-day teeth: dentine and enamel. Like the armored suit of a medieval knight, large plates protected a fish's immobile head, while flexible linked scales covered the rest of its body like chain mail.

A bony external skeleton did more than protect and support a fish. Originally it may have served as a chemical dump and reserve. Calcium and phosphate, the ingredients of bone, are also important ingredients in cell metabolism. They form deposits whenever there is more than the body needs. Whenever calcium and phosphate are not present in the environment and the body needs them, bone is a source of these elements.

When bone began to grow inside the body, it settled in areas that didn't move much, such as the head. The bones of the human skull actually formed from a combination of three distinct bony areas in ancient fish: (1) the bony internal braincase, (2) a bony external surface armor, and (3) bony gill bars.

The internal braincase was originally made of cartilage, a tough yet flexible body tissue that holds its shape. The human nose and ears are also shaped by cartilage. Cartilage cups originally formed around the important sense organs in the fish's head: the eyes, the nostrils, and the semicircular canals. One also surrounded the brain. In time, most of these sense-organ cups fused to the braincase to become one large com-

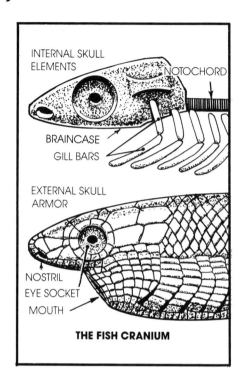

THE FISH CRANIUM

INTERNAL SKULL ELEMENTS
NOTOCHORD
BRAINCASE
GILL BARS
EXTERNAL SKULL ARMOR
NOSTRIL
EYE SOCKET
MOUTH

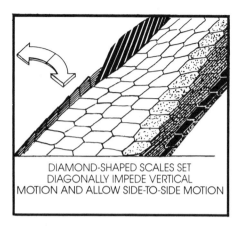

DIAMOND-SHAPED SCALES SET DIAGONALLY IMPEDE VERTICAL MOTION AND ALLOW SIDE-TO-SIDE MOTION

plex structure. Only the eye cups remained movable. Bone, which is tougher than cartilage, replaced it in some cases as the animal matured.

On the surface were scales and plates made up of three layers of material including bone, dentine, and enamel. These scales and plates grew only by depositing more material around their edges, leaving growth rings, similar to those seen in tree trunks. These bones shaped the head like the nose cone of a rocket to slide smoothly through the water.

The gill bars of ancient fish are jointed bones lining and supporting the many gill openings. In humans they evolved to become jaws, tiny middle ear bones, the bone beneath the tongue, and the Adam's apple portion of the voice box.

Along the flexible trunk of the fish's body, diamond-shaped scales, laid like bathroom tiles, improved swimming. They were arranged to permit only side-to-side undulations.

Many primitive fish were sensitive to electric currents. When muscles twitch, they generate minute amounts of electricity. Electrosensory organs in fish helped them find their twitching prey, whether they were in murky waters, buried in sand, or cloaked by darkness.

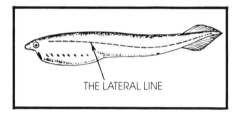

THE LATERAL LINE

The lateral-line system was another useful sense organ in murky waters. It is a series of tiny holes in the skin and scales connected to one another below the skin surface and running in a line from head to tail. The lateral line senses vibrations in the water. Today, fish use it while swimming in schools to avoid crashing into one another.

In living fish, scales often have chemicals called pigments in their cells. Pigments come in many colors. Whiter scales usually appear on the belly, whereas darker ones cover the sides and top. This pattern is called countershading, and it appears on almost every animal that swims. It off-

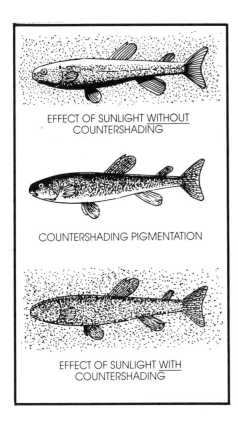

EFFECT OF SUNLIGHT **WITHOUT** COUNTERSHADING

COUNTERSHADING PIGMENTATION

EFFECT OF SUNLIGHT **WITH** COUNTERSHADING

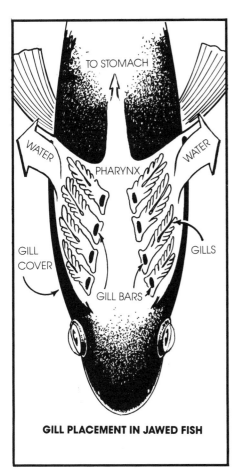

GILL PLACEMENT IN JAWED FISH

sets the natural effects of sunlight and shade on a fish, helping it to blend in with its surroundings. Pigmentation also helps prevent sunburn on fish, the way a tan does on humans.

The exchange of fresh oxygen for stale carbon dioxide took place through the naked skin of early chordates and vertebrates. An armor of scales and plates on some fish prevents this. At the gill openings, oxygen-rich water was always flowing, so that became the natural place for gills to develop. Gills are large feathery tissues full of tiny blood vessels. They are a site of exchange of oxygen and waste gases with the water outside.

In fish with jaws, the gills lie outside the gill bars so that their delicate parts will not be hurt by large prey sliding down the throat. In jawless fish, which do not feed on large prey, gills lie inside the bony arches.

The earliest fish fed upon plankton and bottom debris. As time went on, larger prey was added to the menu. The stomach, an enlarged sac in the intestinal tube, became a holding tank for large prey.

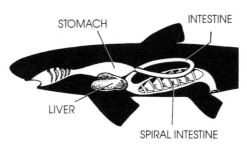

Primitive fish intestines are shaped like a large cigar with a spiral inside. The food goes around and around for better digestion. In higher fishes and land animals, this portion disappears. It is replaced by a simple but very long, meandering tube. In humans, the

intestines reach 27 feet in length.

A liver is present in all animals with a backbone. Its main job is to treat food after it has been digested and prepare the nutrients in food for absorption into the bloodstream. The nearby pancreas produces enzymes that aid in digestion, among other bodily functions.

The spleen is an organ that first appears in fish. It produces, stores, and destroys both red and white blood cells in most vertebrates.

Kidneys first appear as organs in fish. They filter blood for wastes and remove both excess water and salt from the body.

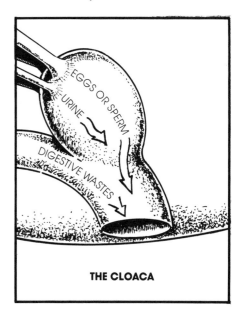

THE CLOACA

The vent, or cloaca (meaning "sewer"), is the common external opening for urine, digestive wastes, eggs, and sperm in fish, amphibians, reptiles, and birds.

It is hard to tell if lower animals sleep or simply become less active at certain hours of the day. With fish it is easier to tell. Most sleep at night, conserving energy until feeding can resume. Fish do not close their eyes because they have no eyelids. There is no indication that fish dream.

The Gnathostome—jaws!...and also paired fins.

Gnathostomes (NATH-oh-stomes), or "jaw mouths," are animals with jaws. Humans are gnathostomes, too. Jaws turned nibbling and sucking fish into predators that could bite. Jaws could dismember large prey. They could also close to prevent small prey from exiting once inside the mouth. Gnathostome fish probably originated in shallow seas but spread rapidly into rivers and lakes.

Teeth originated as sharp scales that wrapped around the rim of the jaws. Their ragged edges helped snare prey. Like shark skin denticles, teeth are made of supertough dentine and enamel. They grow from the inside of the jaws and rotate to, or emerge from, the rim. In ancient fish, teeth appeared in rows along the rim of the jaws, as they do in humans. They also grew from the roof of the mouth and from inside the jaws as well.

Teeth are dulled and worn down with use. As they get old, they are shed and replaced. Sharp new teeth are always coming up.

Gnathostomes developed bony armor much later than did most jawless fish. For a long time these naked speedsters swam in open waters, while their heavily armored jawless relatives cruised the seafloors.

To float or sink in water, a fish has to change its buoyancy, or its weight in relation to that of an equal amount of water. Fish are naturally a little heavier than water. Bony fish developed lungs, simple pockets of tissue just behind the throat. Lungs could be filled with air to make a fish exactly as buoyant as it needed to be. In most modern fish, lungs have evolved to become swim bladders.

The earliest fish could not breathe like a human. It did not have ribs, so it could not inhale. Instead, it gulped air

AN EARLY GNATHOSTOME
PROBABLE ACTUAL SIZE

DORSAL FINS

ANAL FIN

FLESHY FIN FOLDS

PECTORAL FIN

PELVIC FIN

The early gnathostome illustrated here is unknown as a fossil and does not live today. Its design is based on known jawless fish, early sharks, and bony fish.

FIN SPINES

CLIMATIUS
A LATE SILURIAN SPINY SHARK
ACTUAL SIZE

into its throat, then dived headfirst to let the bubble of air rise into its lungs. The fresh air was slowly absorbed by the body, and waste gases filtered out through the skin and gills.

In the earliest finless fish, steering was accomplished by a twist of the head. That changed with the development of fins. An anal fin appeared near the base of the tail. Two dorsal fins grew on the back. A pair of pectoral fins, behind the gills, and pelvic fins, near the cloaca, were steering fins. They also acted like the wings of an airplane, providing lift as the body was driven forward.

Fins began as raised ridges known as fin folds. Cartilage and bone rays developed inside the fins to make them sturdy.

Similar rays of bone originated all along the notochord, chiefly below the dorsal and anal fins. These bones formed the basis for the internal skeleton. Later they became spines on our vertebrae (neck, back, and tail bones.)

Covering the gill openings of bony

What's New?

Jaws
Teeth
Paired fin folds
Bony diamond-shaped scales
Spiracle (primitive eustachian tube)
Interior skeleton
Lungs
Gill covers
Urinary bladder

fish were large plates of bone or cartilage. These gill covers protected the gills and helped the fish pump oxygen-rich water through the gills.

The fish's jaws and gill covers form a double pump system to keep water flowing past the gills, even when the fish itself is not moving. As the mouth opens and the throat deepens, the first pump pulls water in. When the jaws close and the throat rises, water is squeezed back toward the gills. At the same time, the gill covers open, acting like a second pump. This creates suction, which draws water out through the gills to the exterior.

In bony fish, the urinary bladder appears for the first time from a

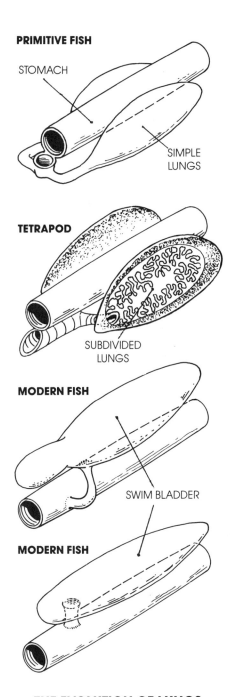

PRIMITIVE FISH

STOMACH

SIMPLE LUNGS

TETRAPOD

SUBDIVIDED LUNGS

MODERN FISH

SWIM BLADDER

MODERN FISH

**THE EVOLUTION OF LUNGS
AND THE SWIM BLADDER**

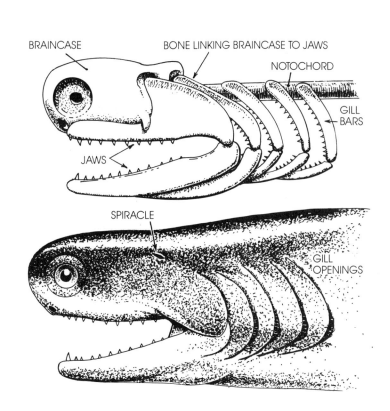

BRAINCASE

BONE LINKING BRAINCASE TO JAWS

NOTOCHORD

GILL BARS

JAWS

SPIRACLE

GILL OPENINGS

HOW THE JAWS EVOLVED

The gill bars in primitive fishes were made up of upper and lower rods. They were hinged in the middle and bent forward. The muscles that pulled these bones together were similar to those that closed the jaws. As the first gill bars enlarged and tilted farther forward, they became increasingly efficient at snaring prey. Finally they became full-fledged jaws lined with jagged rootless teeth.

The second set of gill bars changed to link the jaws to the rear of the braincase. The gill opening that remained between the two sets of gill bars never completely disappeared. It became the spiracle, a tiny opening above the gills still seen in sharks and rays. In amphibians it provided a place for the first eardrum. In humans it remains a part of the hearing apparatus, the eustachian tube. It connects the middle ear to the throat. Sudden pressure changes, the kind that happen when landing or taking off in planes, cause pain in the eardrum. The pain goes away when the eustachian tube opens and relieves the pressure inside the ear.

pinched-off portion of the cloaca. This bag stores urine until the fish is ready to expel it and swim away.

The earliest known fishes with jaws were spiny sharks (illustrated above and not related to real sharks).

They were so named because their fins were supported by hard spines. The spines must have hurt anything that

tried to eat these fish. Human ancestors probably never had such spines. They would have had fin folds instead.

Osteolepis—the fish that breathed through its nose.

If you should ever get a chance to hold a fossil of *Osteolepis* (os-tee-uh-LEE-pus), do so. You will be holding the most ancient fossilized ancestor of humans known to science. Yes, there are fossils that are older than this fish, but they are all offshoots from the direct line of human ancestry. In this book, Ostee is the first proof we have that all the advancements noted so far had indeed taken place.

Ostee was preserved as a fossil because it had a sturdy skeleton, both inside and out. In fact, this fish was named for its "bony scales." A sturdy skeleton is the most important feature an animal must have to live on land. That was the destiny of Ostee's descendents.

Ostee was a freshwater fish. Fresh water is murky from dissolved mud eroding from its banks. It is not as buoyant as seawater because it contains almost no salt. Worst of all, its shallows can easily be warmed by sunlight. Warm water cannot hold enough oxygen for most fish to absorb through their gills.

Murky waters must have limited its vision. Ostee's eyes were rather small. Perhaps this fish "felt" its way around using its electrosensitive skin and lateral-line canals (see pages 40 and 41). Certainly Ostee smelled its way around using its enlarged nasal sacs.

Most jawed fish have 4 nostrils, 2 on each side. Each nasal sac has an entrance and an exit right behind it. In Ostee's case, each exit nostril opened near the eyeballs. This exit would one day become the tear duct in land-living animals.

Ostee is the first fish we know of that could breathe through its nostrils. A new nasal passage, the choana (KO-an-ah), opened into the roof of its mouth. Humans and other animals

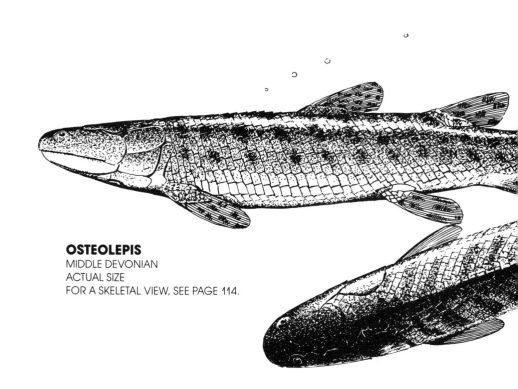

OSTEOLEPIS
MIDDLE DEVONIAN
ACTUAL SIZE
FOR A SKELETAL VIEW, SEE PAGE 114.

that share this trait with *Osteolepis* are called choanates. From Ostee on, nostrils were used for smelling and breathing.

Ostee was a rhipidistian ("fan at the tip" [of the fin]) fish. Related to living coelacanths and lungfish, rhipidistians had sharp teeth, broad muscular fins, and strong skeletons. They were the top predators in the fresh waters of the Devonian period.

Large diamond-shaped scales knitted together with a peg-and-socket arrangement gave Ostee's body great support even in shallow water. Many large bony plates covered its head. The pattern of these plates was identical to that of skull bones in animals with four legs. This is only one of many ways in which Ostee shows its relationship to tetrapods (or "four-footed" creatures).

What's New?

Choana and primitive tear ducts
Electrosensory skin
Larger size
Strong skeleton inside and out
Broad muscular fins
Jointed braincase with palate fangs
Adapted to fresh water

The toughest layer of Ostee's teeth, the enamel layer, folded in on itself like curtain folds. This made each tooth much stronger. Teeth had to be tough to handle scale-studded, armor-plated prey.

A row of teeth lined the edges of Ostee's jaws. Another row emerged on the tongue side of these. Both rows were normal in size. Large fangs emerged from both the palate (the roof of the mouth) and inside the lower jaws. These were its primary weapons. Such fangs were useful for

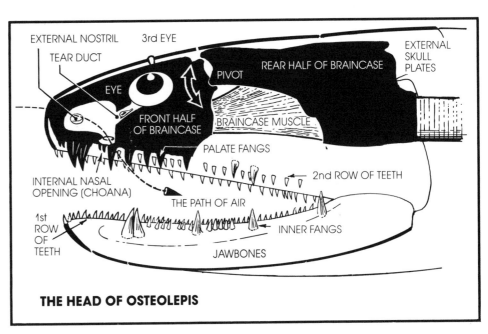

THE HEAD OF OSTEOLEPIS

EXTERNAL NOSTRIL · 3rd EYE · EXTERNAL SKULL PLATES · TEAR DUCT · REAR HALF OF BRAINCASE · PIVOT · EYE · FRONT HALF OF BRAINCASE · BRAINCASE MUSCLE · PALATE FANGS · 2nd ROW OF TEETH · INTERNAL NASAL OPENING (CHOANA) · THE PATH OF AIR · 1st ROW OF TEETH · INNER FANGS · JAWBONES

THE EVOLUTION OF THE PECTORAL FIN

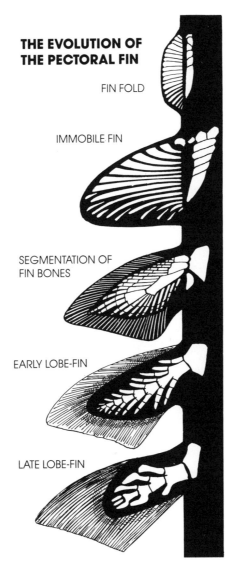

FIN FOLD

IMMOBILE FIN

SEGMENTATION OF FIN BONES

EARLY LOBE-FIN

LATE LOBE-FIN

THE EVOLUTION OF THE SKULL IN LOBE-FIN FISH AND A TETRAPOD

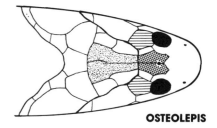

OSTEOLEPIS

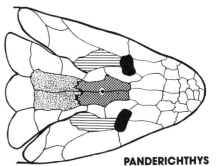

PANDERICHTHYS

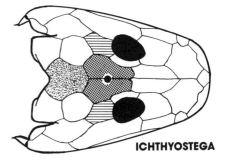

ICHTHYOSTEGA

piercing the hard, thick scales of other fish.

Part of the power to drive those fangs came from a special muscle that snapped the front half of Ostee's braincase down like a stapler. The space between the two halves of the braincase is the same space or "soft spot" a human baby has between its skull bones before they knit together.

To help dislodge prey impaled on its fangs, Ostee had a stiff, bony tongue in the bowl of its mouth.

Ostee lived during the middle and late Devonian periods in Scotland, Antarctica, and Northern Asia. At that time these places were tropical. Ostee is one of the earliest rhipidistians known from a complete skeleton. Currently, older relatives are known only from a scattering of broken pieces.

Gyroptychius—a larger size put more on the menu.

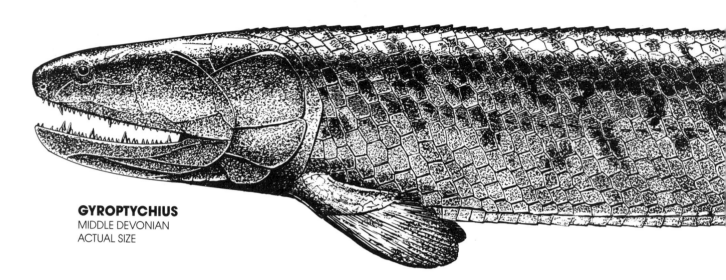

GYROPTYCHIUS
MIDDLE DEVONIAN
ACTUAL SIZE

What's New?

Larger overall size
Long straight tail
Dorsal fins smaller and shifted
 to the rear
Lobes containing jointed bones
 corresponding to limb bones
Hipbones
Eyeball bones

Gyroptychius (jy-rop-TIK-ee-us) was named for the "encircling folds" of its bony scales. It looked like, and probably behaved like, living garfish. These are large, ferocious, North American predators that prefer quiet, weedy, and stagnant backwater areas.

A close relative of *Osteolepis* (see page 44), Gyro was large enough to have given a human a nasty bite. Everything from insects to shellfish and large fish was probably on this fish's menu.

Compared to *Osteolepis*, Gyro's top fins were smaller and shifted to the rear. They helped the tail to increase Gyro's speed.

Gyro's cylindrical body was up to 18 inches long and armored with thick bony scales. It would have resembled a beached log waiting in ambush in the shallows. Gyro thrived in muddy water. This fish survived in ditches and pools that were so small and shallow, there was hardly any room at all

to turn around in. The fact that it breathed air made this possible. In fact, fossils of this and other rhipidistian fish are usually found in mass graves at the base of drought-stricken ponds. It seems obvious that such fish were not able to crawl to new water holes during droughts.

Rather than bending up at the tip, Gyro's tail went straight out. It was an adaptation to shallow water. It helped the tail avoid the drying effects of air above the surface. Youngsters lived in even shallower waters to avoid predators. They had even longer muscular tails. The long thick tails of primitive amphibians (see pages 50-51) evolved from the tails of these fish.

Stronger skeletons of bone developed in some rhipidistians as their size increased. In some species, a column of jointed bones appeared within the lobes of each fin. The structure of these bones is close to that of the limb bones of all animals that live

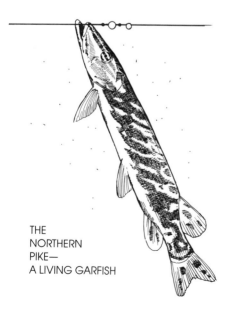

THE
NORTHERN
PIKE—
A LIVING GARFISH

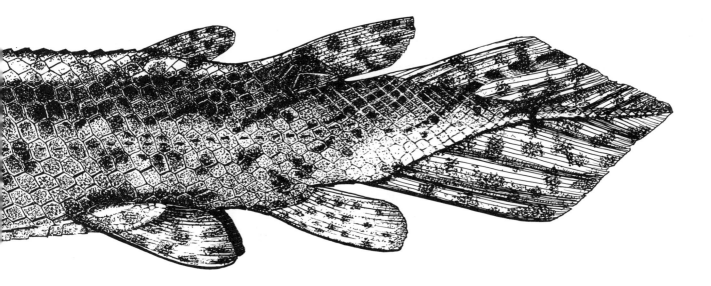

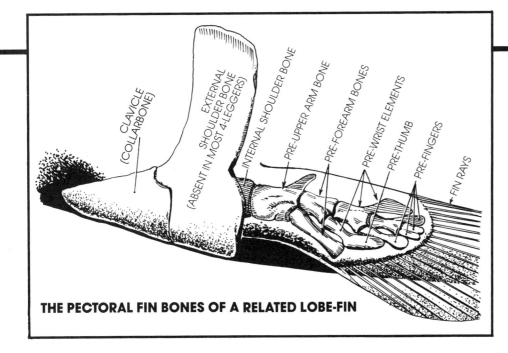

THE PECTORAL FIN BONES OF A RELATED LOBE-FIN

CLAVICLE (COLLARBONE)

EXTERNAL SHOULDER BONE (ABSENT IN MOST 4-LEGGERS)

INTERNAL SHOULDER BONE

PRE-UPPER ARM BONE

PRE-FOREARM BONES

PRE-WRIST ELEMENTS

PRE-THUMB

PRE-FINGERS

FIN RAYS

on land, including humans (see illustration).

Shoulder blades and a pelvis formed a base for the front and rear pairs of fins. Joined to each base was a single bone corresponding to the single upper armbones and thighbones of four-leggers. Following these was a joint, corresponding to the elbow and knee joints. Next in line were a pair of bones, side by side, similar to the two bones of the forearm and of the calf. Then there was another joint, like the wrist and ankle joint. Smaller pairs of bones and joints followed, and these correspond to certain wrist, ankle, fin-ger, and toe bones in four-legged animals. At the end of the lobe, dozens of tiny bony filaments fanned out to form the finny portion of the lobe-fin.

In the shallowest water, the shoulder and pelvic fins had different jobs to do. The fore fin's main job was support, keeping the fish's weight off its lungs. The hind fins were better at pushing.

Gyro was like most vertebrates (except jawless fish and mammals) because within each of its eyeballs was a ring of bones supporting them. This ring helped keep the eyeball's shape when the fish moved into the greater pressure of deeper water. It also may have helped focus images.

Gyro is known from fossils found in freshwater deposits in east Greenland, Norway, and Scotland. During the middle Devonian period, these areas formed a single large island on a planet that was otherwise almost completely under water.

Panderichthys—a fish that was losing its fins.

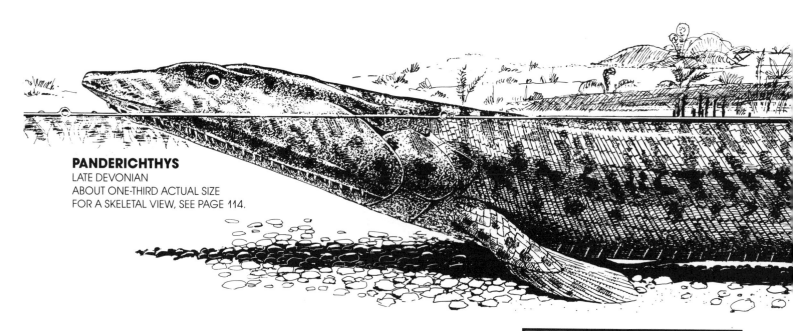

PANDERICHTHYS
LATE DEVONIAN
ABOUT ONE-THIRD ACTUAL SIZE
FOR A SKELETAL VIEW, SEE PAGE 114.

Try to think of the famous Florida walking catfish when you read about *Panderichthys* (pan-der-IK-this), named for the German fossil-scientist C. H. Pander. Keeping in mind the catfish, you will get a good idea about this peculiar animal.

Pan was not a speedy swimmer. The tail fin was short and slender. The dorsal and anal fins had disappeared. Either they had withered away or they had merged with the diminishing tail fin.

Pan lived in a coastal area, perhaps near the mud flats of a river delta. It was almost certainly a shallows wader. This fish may also have crawled overland to other bodies of water, seeking food, mating partners, or simply a wet place during a drought.

Although this fish had gills, Pan was probably able to survive in wet or rainy surroundings for a day or more completely out of water.

Pan had the body, fins, and jaws of a fish, but the skull was flattened and shaped like that of a four-legged amphibian. This rhipidistian was flatter than any of its relatives and could stay submerged in the shallowest of puddles, protected from the sun's drying rays. Staying as low as possible was the only means of hauling its muscular but otherwise unsupported body across the mud flats. The center of balance stayed low, which helped it avoid toppling over while wriggling over mud and beaches.

In time, Pan's relatives came to rely more and more upon their enlarged muscular fins to get from place to place. These fins also took some weight off the chest, enabling Pan's lungs to fill with air.

When this walking fish left its home puddle behind, it also left water's natural buoyancy behind. On land Pan had a weight problem!

Large ribs extended from each back vertebra to help support Pan's internal organs from the crush of gravity. The ribs were large in relation to those of other fish, but they were small in relation to those of four-footed animals.

When breathing air, Pan depended on its throat muscles to force air back into its lungs. You can still see this ancient form of inhaling when you watch frogs breathe. The lungs acted like rubber balloons. Every time they stopped filling, they deflated.

What's New?

Shallows wader/overland crawler
Larger overall size
Flattened body and skull
Textured skull bones
Eyes on top of skull
Nostrils at edge of jawline
Smaller scales
Electrosensory scale layer disappears
Enlarged ribs
Enlarged forefins
Short and slender tail fin
Dorsal and anal fins disappear

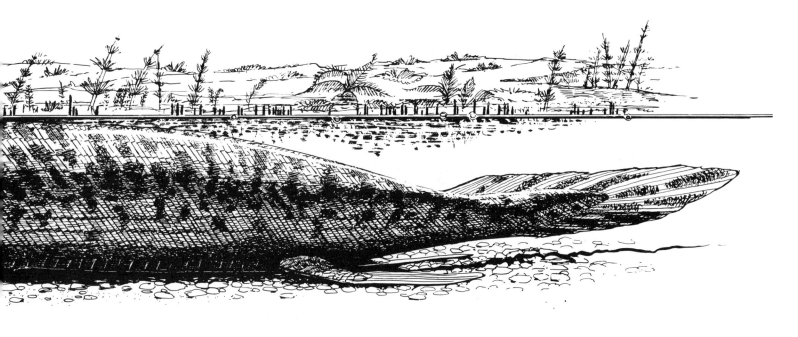

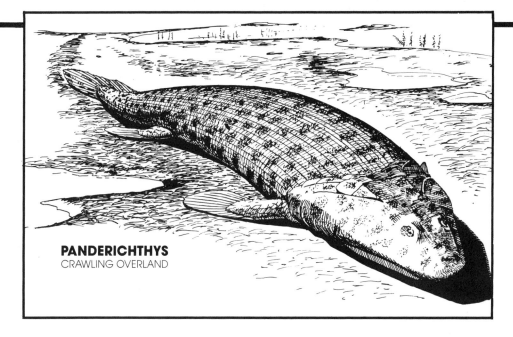

PANDERICHTHYS
CRAWLING OVERLAND

Pan's skull bones were textured with ridges and valleys. Prehistoric flat-headed amphibians and living crocodiles are other animals with similar skull decorations. These pits and peaks evidently provide strength to flattened skulls.

A double row of sharp teeth plus palate fangs suggest that Pan was still a fierce predator. At 4 feet long, this fish would have been the largest land animal living at that time.

Despite the great number of characteristics tying panderichthyids with amphibians, Pan was not the direct ancestor, only a close relative. Pan's fin bones did not end in finger branches, and its skull was probably much too flat. Pan's body was a bit too long, and the rear fins a bit too small.

Panderichthys lived 365 million years ago during the late Devonian period, in what is now Russia. A close relative comes from Quebec. At that time both of those places were equatorial and not as far from one another as they are now.

Pan's scales were smaller than those of other rhipidistians. Although Pan lost the layer in those scales that made them sensitive to minute electrical impulses, the lateral-line system remained intact.

Like primitive amphibians (see page 50) and the living mudskipper (a fish that spends part of each day on mud flats), Pan's eyes were placed on top of its flat head. Perhaps what appeared above the surface was more important to see than what swam below. Perhaps Pan stayed on the pond bottom and watched for prey that swam above.

Pan's nostrils were located at the very edge of its jawline and they faced downward. The very first tetrapods had nostrils like these.

Ichthyostega—a fishlike amphibian with four on the floor.

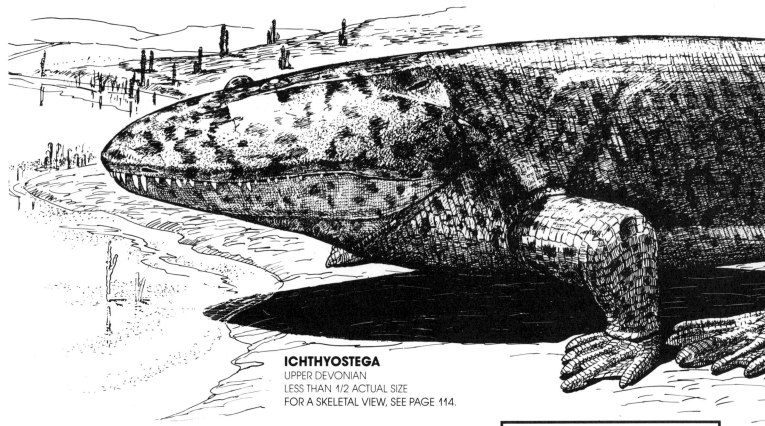

ICHTHYOSTEGA
UPPER DEVONIAN
LESS THAN 1/2 ACTUAL SIZE
FOR A SKELETAL VIEW, SEE PAGE 114.

What's New?

Legs, feet, and toes
Fins disappear from limbs
Solidified skull
Shoulder girdle detached from skull
Enlarged pelvis, with attachment to
    backbone
Enlarged and overlapping ribs
Interconnecting vertebrae
Long tail
Eardrums
Gill covers much reduced
Teeth along edge of jaws larger
Probable:
    Vocal cords
    Incompletely divided heart
    Three eyelids
    Salivary glands
    Tear glands
    Fleshy tongue

About 360 million years ago, on the mud flats, sandbars, and riverbanks of steamy equatorial eastern Greenland, there emerged a creature that could both walk on land and swim in water. It had 4 well-developed limbs. They had evolved from the fleshy lobe-fins of its ancestors. Each limb ended in webbed feet that had 5 to 7 toes. With a sturdy internal skeleton it was able to hoist its belly off the ground. *Ichthyostega* (ik-thee-OS-teg-uh), named for the "fishlike roof" of its skull, is the earliest well-known tetrapod. Humans are also tetrapods.

Panderichthys's fins pointed toward the rear (see pages 48 and 49). Ikky's feet pointed forward, in the direction of travel. Recently discovered late Devonian footprints from Australia point out to the sides. The creature

that left these was an evolutionary link with even more primitive legs than those of Ikky.

Lobe-fins and amphibians may have lived in such weed-choked waters that crawling on land was not much more difficult than crawling through soggy swamp plants. On the other hand, amphibians may have become good at walking over dry land because they were trying to stay wet. If their home pond dried up, they had to find another. Those with better legs survived. Amphibians know where to find water because they can smell it and they follow their noses.

When the mating season came, females would croak to attract suitors. Upon hearing them, males in other ponds would try to reach them. The one that fertilized the eggs probably

WALKING GAIT

had the best legs.

Walking on dry land was not without its rewards. There would have been plenty of walking fish to eat, as well as insects, scorpions, centipedes, and millipedes. Perhaps this was the main reason Ikky evolved legs.

As an amphibian (or "double-life being"), Ikky laid hundreds of eggs in the water. The hatchlings probably resembled small adults, but with fern-like external gills for breathing.

Ikky's legs were very much like those of living animals. Evidently evo-lution from fins had been quite rapid. The bones and muscles in Ikky's limbs, hips, and shoulders were big and stout to handle the burden of its weight out of water. Ikky's legs hardly moved at all back and forth. Their main job was to lift the belly off the ground.

Forward motion came from the backbone snaking from side to side to advance one side of the shoulders and pelvis forward and then the other. Ikky's legs stuck straight out to the sides, in a push-up posture. The feet

were far enough from Ikky's backbone to give each stride a big arc. They were not so far that the strain to keep them up was unbearable.

In many other ways, Ikky was leaving its aquatic ancestry behind. Its gill covers were greatly reduced, suggesting that its gills had virtually disappeared. Ikky's skull was a solid structure without movable sections as in fish. Only the jaws remained mobile.

A solid skull and a longer snout made the "stapler" method of biting used by the lobe-fins less effective (see page 45). That is why there is no trace of braincase muscles in Ikky's head, although unlike all other four-leggers, the braincase did remain in 2 immovable parts. Ikky had no palate fangs (one of the factors removing this

Ichthyostega—continued.

DIRECTION OF TRAVEL

FOOT
HAND
FOOT
HAND
FOOT
HAND
FOOT
HAND

THE FIRST FOOTPRINTS

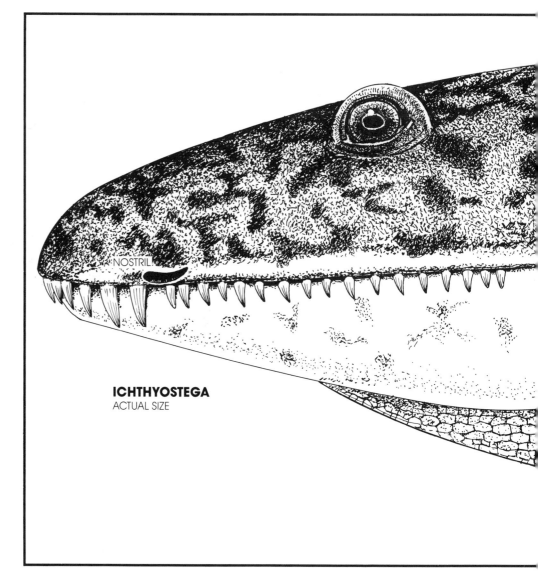

NOSTRIL

ICHTHYOSTEGA
ACTUAL SIZE

amphibian from direct human ancestry), but the double row of edge teeth that remained were larger.

With reduced gill covers, the shoulder girdle was separated from the skull. Ikky's shoulder bones wrapped around the enlarged rib cage. The pelvis and one set of ribs made a solid connection. With its weight supported by these braces, Ikky could rest on the mud flats without crushing its lungs beneath its own bulk.

Before Ikky's backbone became completely adapted to load lifting, the main support of the torso came from Ikky's unusual ribs. Unlike those of almost all other animals, these ribs had huge extensions that overlapped one another. They protected their contents like a large mailing tube or armadillo plates.

Ikky's backbone was stronger because each vertebra linked with its neighbors. However, each vertebra was still made of several small pieces wrapping themselves around the thick notochord.

Air-breathing animals need one circulatory system for their lungs and one for the rest of their body. In tetrapods, the heart is divided to handle both jobs. However, in amphibians and primitive reptiles, the division remains incomplete. The blood that is circulated to the body is never completely refreshed the way it is in more

active animals.

Most tetrapods, from frogs to dogs, are able to retract their eyeballs into their sockets to moisten or protect them. If eyeballs dry out, they cloud up. Every time amphibian eyes are pulled in, lids automatically close over. Tiny tear glands provide the needed "windshield-washer fluid." A third clear eyelid is present as well. It is inside the other two, to protect the eyes without cutting off vision. This special membrane is found today in most birds and reptiles, as well as in some mammals, such as dogs.

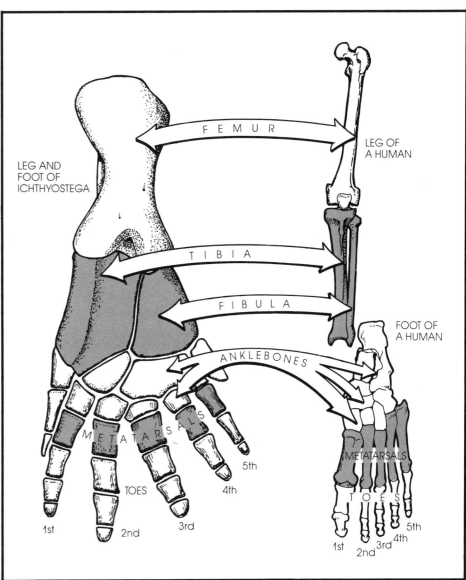

Lateral lines, those water-vibration detectors, were still prominent on Ikky's skull. Ikky must have spent part of each day underwater.

There was a notch at the back of Ikky's skull that formed around the spiracle opening (see page 43). Ikky probably breathed air through this hole while keeping the rest of its body submerged. The hole probably had a movable flap of skin over it serving as a cover. In many later amphibians this flap became an eardrum. With this primitive eardrum Ikky might have heard only loud, deep sounds, such as croaks. If Ikky could have heard croaks, perhaps this ancestor of the bullfrog could have made them as well with newly developed vocal cords.

At 3 feet in length, Ikky had few enemies under the water and none on land. To eat food on dry land this predator needed some sort of lubricant to help a meal slide down its throat. Salivary glands make watery saliva to lubricate the mouth. These glands become especially active right before an animal is about to eat.

Ikky's tail was long and muscular, but some fishy fin rays still remained at the tip. Long, heavy tails are useful to tetrapods. A tail acts as a counterweight in back of the hips to keep the backbone arched and the belly off the ground.

Large, bony V-shaped scales covered Ikky's belly, protecting it against scraping. Bony scales do not seal in moisture, so early amphibians probably ventured out on land only at night, in shade, or on overcast days. Even today most amphibians prefer night to day and damp to dry.

Gephyrostegus—a lizardlike amphibian.

GEPHYROSTEGUS AND YOUNG
LATE CARBONIFEROUS
ACTUAL SIZE
FOR A SKELETAL VIEW, SEE PAGE 115.

What's New?

Smaller overall size
Slender limbs
Long toes
Reptile shape
Neck
Tiny circular scales
Skeletal muscles improved
Slender ribs assisting in breathing
Sturdier backbone
Notochord reduced to a thread
  and disks
Huge eyes
Boxlike head
Nostrils at tip of snout
One row of marginal teeth
Slender sensitive ear bone
Lateral line disappears
Gill covers absent

Most of the known prehistoric amphibians seemed to spend more time in water than on dry land. Some of these types developed huge heads, long bodies, and snaky tails. Some had no use for legs, so they lost them. There was at least one exception that became even better adapted to life on dry land, and that was *Gephyrostegus* (jeff-ih-ROS-teg-us), named for the "bridgelike roof" of its skull.

Smaller than most of its contemporaries, Geffy was a miniature souped-up version of *Ichthyostega*. While its relative had been thick, like a fish, Geffy was slender, like a lizard. That is because its muscles and bones had improved and they supported only a fraction of the weight.

Geffy's days in the water were over. As an adult, Geffy had no fins on its tail. The skull bore no trace of lateral-line grooves (used to sense water-borne vibrations), and Geffy had no gill covers.

Perhaps Geffy could swim by kicking with its huge froglike feet. More likely, its 5 toes were long to give each stride the maximum push and to prevent slipping while Geffy scooted over fallen moss-covered coal forest logs. The longest toe on each of its "hands" and feet was the fourth one, the "ring finger" in humans. The others became progressively shorter toward the "thumb" and first toe. As seen in the illustration above, that arrangement allowed them to clear the ground during the forward swing of each stride.

The notochord canal in Geffy's backbones was quite a bit smaller. The thick notochord that had once made swimmers out of burrowers was being phased out. In Geffy's back it remained only as a slender thread through each vertebra and as a disk between each pair. In humans, a "slipped disk" is really a slipped notochord segment.

Geffy had huge eyes, perhaps for seeing insect prey. They were positioned on the sides of its head rather than on top. That is because the skull was considerably less flattened.

Geffy's nostrils had moved forward to the tip of its snout, where they could be poked into burrows and smelly things. This is where they remain today in most four-legged animals and

humans.

The ear bone connecting Geffy's eardrum to its braincase was much more slender than that of *Ichthyostega*. It was more sensitive to a wider range of sounds such as whistles and chirps.

Tiny circular bony scales covered Geffy's body everywhere except on the chest and belly. A series of large V-shaped scales protected that area from chafing.

Geffy's mobile neck helped aim its mouth at insect prey. The ribs were normal in appearance. That meant that Geffy's rib muscles were probably able to expand and contract to draw air in and out of its lungs. This was a new way of breathing, and it is still practiced by humans.

If Geffy looked so much like a reptile, why isn't it considered one? Scientists have observed that reptiles have no continuous notochord and their backbones connect to one another more strongly than Geffy's did. In addition,

TOE LENGTH DEPENDS ON TOE CLEARANCE DURING EACH STRIDE

although only one row of teeth lined the margins of Geffy's jaws, a few small palate fangs still persisted. No reptiles have these fangs. Geffy's head was large, like that of most other amphibians. The top of the skull was flat at the back and angled to form "horns," pointed parts above the eardrums. These were attachment points for the large muscles needed to hold up the heavy head. Since early reptiles have no eardrum frames on their skull, they do not have these "horns."

Fossils of young Geffys have been found. They have all the features of an adult, but with youthful proportions (a bigger head and eyes). Like many a living salamander, Geffy's legs must have developed within a short time, either before or after hatching underwater.

Fossils of gephyrostegids are known only from the early and late Carboniferous periods, 320 to 300 million years ago, in Western Europe and eastern North America. At that time both were neighboring portions of a single continent.

Hylonomus—parents and eggs were dry on the outside but

The chordates that have membrane-coated eggs are the reptiles, birds, and mammals. They are called amniotes because one of the egg membranes is the amnion. The amnion forms a minipond for the embryo to develop in. It's as wet as a pond but contains no aquatic egg and tadpole eaters.

The outermost egg layer is the shell. The shell is tough enough to resist tiny predators and protects its contents from drying out in the hot sun. It may be leathery, like a snake's egg, or brittle, like a bird's. It is tough to break into an amniote's egg. It is tough to break out, too. Bird and turtle hatchlings have an egg tooth, a hard temporary growth on their snout. They use it to cut through the membranes and shell. Shortly after hatching, the egg tooth falls off.

Living reptiles and mammals have separate ancestries dating back at least as far as the late Carboniferous period, 310 million years ago, yet both have eggs layered with similar membranes. We assume that a common ancestor began laying membrane-coated eggs before reptiles and mammals went their separate ways.

When eggs became membrane coated, fertilization had to take place before they reached the membrane-coating glands inside the female. The most primitive living reptile, the tuatara, provides an example of how early reptiles practiced internal fertilization. The male has no sperm-delivery organ, so he simply presses his cloaca against the female's during mating.

Exactly when membrane-coated eggs were first laid cannot be determined directly from fossil skeletons. Indirect evidence, however, provides certain clues.

There are living salamanders that lay eggs on land, similar to reptiles. The young hatch out as miniatures of their parents. Their eggs have larger than usual yolks to feed them until they are fully developed. Without a special membrane for support, these jellylike eggs must remain tiny or risk falling apart. The largest salamanders that lay such eggs only reach 4 inches in length as adults. Lizards of this size lay similar-sized eggs.

Owing to the tiny size of the eggs they laid, the first reptiles grew to be no more than 4 inches long. They lived 338 million years ago.

Hylonomus (hie-LON-oh-muss) was 3 times as long and lived a few million years later than the earliest known reptiles. Although it was larger, it was still built along the same lines as those early types. Hy found shelter in the base of a tree-fern stump hollowed out by rot and forest fire. That is why it was named "wood district."

In its skeleton and body proportions, Hy was as slender as a living fence lizard. This early reptile was built for clambering over obstacles, such as rocks and fallen tree limbs. Instead of passively waiting for prey to crawl or fly by, Hy probably scampered after them. Two pairs of ribs were attached to its pelvis for greater support.

In contrast to lizardlike amphibians, Hy had a small head, only one row of teeth on the jawline, and no palate fangs. These features suggest that Hy lived on insects, perhaps dining on one that is still with us—the cockroach. A new row of teeth spanning the back of the palate made sure a meal didn't wiggle free as it was bolted down the throat without chewing.

The notch at the rear of gephyrostegid skulls (see page 54) left

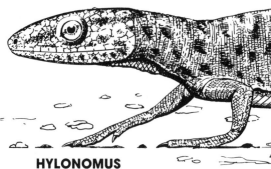

HYLONOMUS
LATE CARBONIFEROUS
ACTUAL SIZE
FOR A SKELETAL VIEW, SEE PAGE 115.

a space for an eardrum, but Hy's skull had no such notch. Hy's ear bone was also quite large. Like a snake, Hy may not have been able to hear airborne sounds very well. This reptile could have felt the approach of footsteps, however, by the vibrations they sent through the ground or the log on which it rested. Hy's most sensitive sound sensors were its lower jawbones. Like snakes, turtles, and lizards, Hy probably did not croak or chirp.

The only scales that Hy had with bone in them protected the belly. Unlike fish scales made of bone, reptile scales are made of keratin, a horny substance that usually does not fossilize. Human fingernails are made of keratin. Reptile claws, which appear at this time, are made of keratin over bone. Keratin seals in moisture. Hy probably had keratin scales on its head, legs, back, and tail. Like living lizards, Hy liked to warm up under a bright sun. Its keratin scales protected this reptile from drying out.

Like all vertebrates, reptiles can only live in a limited range of temperatures. Because they are cold-blooded, they can not regulate their temperature from within. Instead, they move to

stayed moist on the inside.

EGG

What's New?

- Smaller head
- Smaller overall size
- Slender limbs
- Stronger backbone
- Solid vertebrae
- Two pairs of ribs connect to pelvis
- One row of edge teeth disappears and one remains
- Palate fangs absent
- Back-of-palate teeth appear
- Hearing by bone conduction only
- Probable:
  - Amniotic egg
  - Keratin scales
  - Internal fertilization
  - Navel (belly button)
  - Insect diet
  - Sunbathing

THE PALATE OF HYLONOMUS

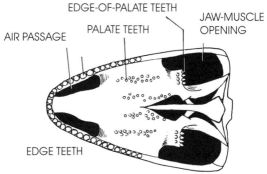

EDGE-OF-PALATE TEETH

JAW-MUSCLE OPENING

PALATE TEETH

AIR PASSAGE

EDGE TEETH

a more comfortable spot when they can. In extreme weather they seek shelter. But if it's sunny and warm, they are usually found basking out in the open.

The Amniote Egg

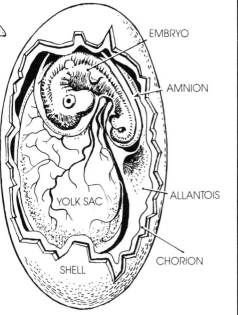

EMBRYO

YOLK SAC →

AMPHIBIAN

EMBRYO

AMNION

YOLK SAC

ALLANTOIS

SHELL

CHORION

REPTILE (AMNIOTE)

The embryos of both amphibians and reptiles are attached to a yolk sac, the primary food supply for the developing embryo. In reptiles the yolk sac is much larger because it will be used for a longer time. Its attachment point remains on the hatchling as the navel, or belly button.

The embryo and its yolk develop in a fluid-filled sac, the amnion. It serves as a replica of an ancestral pond. The allantois (e-LAN-to-is) is a sac covered with blood vessels attached to the intestine. It acts as a bladder and as a breathing organ. The allantois and the outermost membrane, the chorion (KO-ri-on), together operate as a lung surface.

Hundreds of eggs are laid in a typical amphibian batch. Predators eat most of the babies, leaving only a few lucky survivors.

Reptiles produce fewer but larger and better-protected eggs. Each hatchling comes out fully formed and ready to fend for itself. Today many of these babies also fall prey to predators. During the Carboniferous period, however, there were few predators in the high and dry places where reptiles made their nests.

The Amniotes—the egg came first.

The chart to the right is an overview of the family tree of amniotes from 320 million years ago to the present. Amniotes include mammals, birds, reptiles, and their ancestors. All of these animals had embryos protected with a number of membranes, one of which is the amnion (see page 56).

At the same time that reptiles were first emerging, other reptilelike animals also appeared. It is difficult to classify some of these as either reptiles or amphibians. Some were among the first plant eaters; others were toothy predators. They all had heavy bones and sprawling limbs. These reptile/amphibians survived for 50 million years before finally becoming extinct.

The first undisputed reptiles resembled *Hylonomus* (see page 56). Shortly after they began laying membrane-coated eggs, a rift began to appear, separating the synapsid reptiles from the sauropsid reptiles. Mammals trace their ancestry through the synapsid branch (described in detail in the following chapters).

The sauropsid branch includes all of the remaining living reptiles, as well as dinosaurs and birds. With the exception of the large plant-eating pareiasaurs, or "wall lizards," which grew to the size of cattle, most sauropsids of the Permian period remained small insect eaters. They lived under the domination of the much larger synapsids.

About 248 million years ago something happened that killed 90 percent or more of all the animals then living. This event marked the end of the Paleozoic era and ushered in the Mesozoic era, starting with the Triassic period. The synapsid clan lost their dominance, but did not disappear. The surviving sauropsids quickly repopulated the planet.

The ichthyosaurs (IK-thee-uh-sores), or "fish lizards," made the sea their home. Their limbs became paddles, and their tails became tail fins.

Turtles developed a shelter of hard plates and expanded ribs called a shell. They had a beak in place of teeth.

Except for turtles, all living reptiles, dinosaurs, and birds are diapsids. Diapsids have 4 holes in their skull behind the eye sockets. One pair opens on top, and another hole pierces each cheek.

The plesiosaurs ("near lizards") and their kin began as divers. Later types used their broad paddles, much as penguins use their wings, to "fly" underwater. The related placodonts ("plate-toothed") were armored divers. Their teeth were shaped like paving stones to crush clams and oysters.

Most lizards and their kin remained small insect eaters. One group, however, were seagoing giants up to 50 feet long. Snakes are lizard descendants that have lost their legs. The tuatara is the sole surviving member of a lizardlike group that became virtually extinct millions of years ago.

Archosaurs (ARK-uh-sores), or "ruling reptiles," were the top predators on land during the entire Mesozoic era. Most can be identified by an additional hole in the lower jaws as well as one in the snout region of the skull.

Archosaur kin include unusual reptiles that looked like lizards, but their ankle bones indicate their true kinship with the archosaurs.

Early archosaurs had bony plates in the skin of their back, the same as in living crocodiles. Early archosaurs also had legs that varied in posture between sprawling and nearly erect.

Some archosaurs were able to stand on their fully erect hind legs alone. A stiff neck and erect hind legs allowed some archosaurs to breathe while sprinting, something that undulating lizards cannot do. Pterosaurs (TARE-uh-sores), or "winged lizards," are archosaurs that developed wings and learned to fly.

Erect legs can support weight more easily than sprawling limbs can. Some dinosaurs, or "terrible lizards," grew to be giants. The meat eaters always remained close to the design of the first dinosaurs. Some small meat eaters became birds when they grew feathers. Birds are living dinosaurs.

Sauropods were dinosaurs with long necks able to reach high plants. Most became so top-heavy, they dropped back down to all fours.

The other plant-eating dinosaurs had a beak and special hipbones that allowed their bellies to expand rearward. Some of these were armored with plates of bone, whereas others had horns and other means for defense.

By the end of the Cretaceous period the giant reptiles were in decline. Many became extinct 65 million years ago, perhaps as a result of a global period of darkness and cold brought on by the collision of a giant meteor with Earth. As soon as the "terrible lizards" were out of the picture, the surviving mammals and birds began to repopulate the planet.

From the Permian through the Jurassic periods, all of Earth's continents were together in one supercontinent. That enabled dinosaurs and mammals to spread around the world.

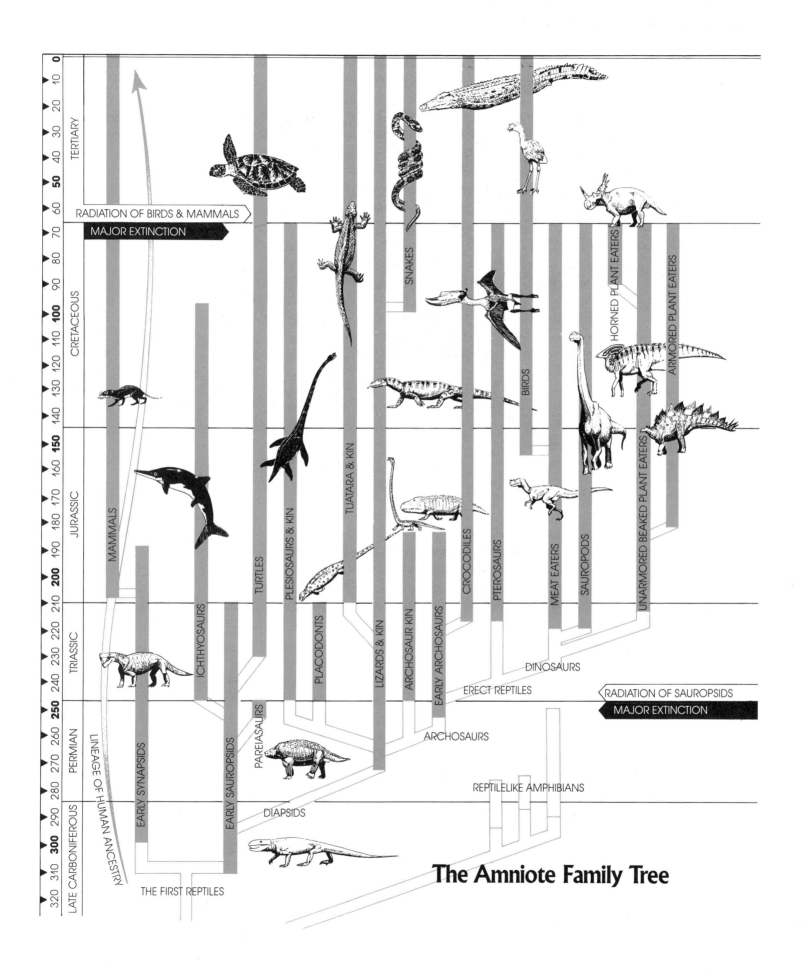

The Amniote Family Tree

Archaeothyris—had fangs and a hole in its head.

What's New?

Synapsid opening in skull
Larger overall size
Proportionately larger head
Larger teeth, including canine fangs
Down slope to rear of skull and
 jawline
Larger limbs
Shorter toes

The origin of mammals begins with the iguana-sized reptile *Archaeothyris* (ar-kee-AH-thih-rus), or "ancient opening." Arky had only one feature to connect it to mammals. It was an opening in the skull behind the eye socket.

This hole, called the synapsid opening, is also found in the human skull. It is the space between the cheekbone and the braincase. The word synapsid means "joined arch." It refers to the cheekbone below this hole, which is often arched in mammals. In Arky, this hole served to rechannel the force of each bite through skull bone instead of through skull joints.

Except for its synapsid opening, Arky was an ordinary reptile, only big-ger than its contemporaries. Arky had a stronger skeleton, larger limbs, and shorter toes than other reptiles of its time. It probably ate large prey such as fish, amphibians, and other reptiles. Arky had larger teeth, including some that were enlarged to fangs. It also had a larger head and jaws than those of insect eaters.

Arky had a jawline that sloped down toward the rear, matching the slope at the back of the skull. In this way Arky's jaw muscles pulled the jaws closed and to the rear as well. This was important because otherwise Arky's jaws might have become dislocated in attempts to tear chunks of meat from large carcasses.

Arky lived 300 million years ago, during the late Carboniferous period in Nova Scotia, Canada. At that time it was a tropical coal forest swamp. Arky was one of the earliest pelycosaurs, the first major group of synapsid reptiles. There are pelycosaur fragments from 10 million years earlier, which is probably close to the origin of the synapsids.

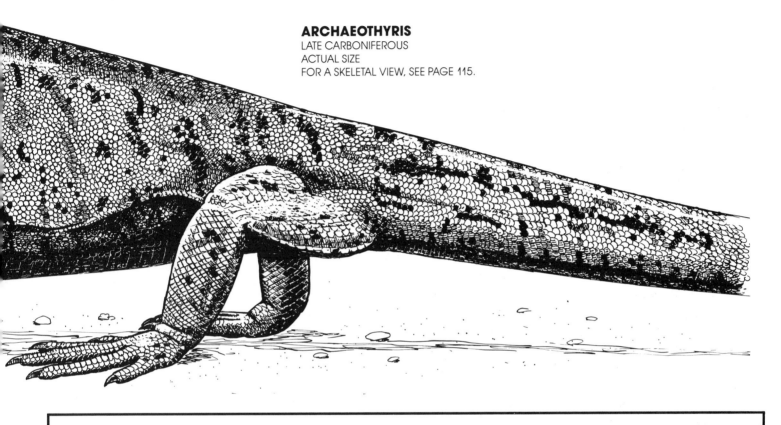

ARCHAEOTHYRIS
LATE CARBONIFEROUS
ACTUAL SIZE
FOR A SKELETAL VIEW, SEE PAGE 115.

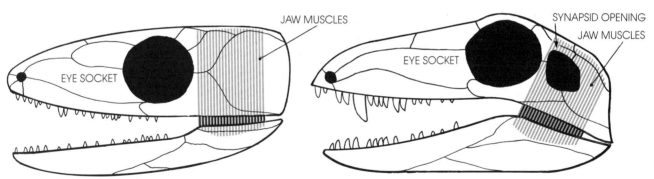

THE SKULLS OF HYLONOMUS AND ARCHAEOTHYRIS

Insects do not put up much of a struggle when bitten, so *Hylonomus* jaw muscles simply closed the jaws straight up, like a drawbridge. Hy's teeth were small, like those of modern insect-eating lizards.

Archaeothyris, on the other hand, had jaw muscles arranged at an angle. The jaws were pulled back with almost as much force as they were pulled up. Otherwise, struggling prey,

fighting against large teeth might have pulled Arky's jaw out of its socket. The synapsid opening shifted biting stresses through the skull bones themselves, away from the weaker joints between them.

The Synapsids—masters of the Permian.

The chart to the right is an overview of the first two-thirds of the family tree of synapsids (defined in previous entry). Synapsids began as ordinary reptiles that adapted to eating larger prey. In time they changed into a variety of shapes and sizes. But as reptiles, none had fins or wings, or became two-legged runners.

Three waves of synapsids appear in the fossil record.

The first wave included the pelycosaurs ("basin [hip] lizards"), low-slung reptiles that held their elbows and knees in a perpetual push-up posture, like a lizard. Most fossils come from the American Southwest.

The second wave included the therapsids (or "beast arch" [cheekbones]). They were much more mammal-like reptiles that raised themselves higher off the ground by holding their elbows and knees down at an angle. Most fossils come from South Africa and Russia.

The third wave includes the mammals (named for their milk glands), many of which place their feet directly beneath their bodies in a completely erect posture.

The first pelycosaurs were ophiacodonts ("snake teeth"), meat eaters that probably stayed near the water. Large-bellied plant-eating caseids (named for fossil scientist E. C. Case) roamed the higher elevations. Plant-eating edaphosaurs ("dirt lizards") had a raised sail of skin and bone on their backs. Sphenacodont ("wedge teeth") sailbacks were the largest predators on land. Sphenacodonts without sails were the ancestors of the more advanced therapsids.

Therapsids were more numerous, and became more widespread and varied than pelycosaurs had been. Dicynodonts ("two dog-teeth") were plant eaters that had lost almost all of their teeth. In place of teeth they developed turtle-like beaks. Dinocephalians ("terrible-headed ones") had thick skulls, which they used to ram one another as well as enemies. Most gorgonopsians ("gorgon-faced ones") and therocephalians ("beast-headed ones") were wolflike meat eaters with huge fangs. Some, however, ate plants.

Most of the therapsids became extinct during the Permian/Triassic catastrophe, an event that wiped out 90 percent of the species then living. A few somehow survived.

Cynodonts ("dog teeth") were dog-to rat-sized therapsids. Some of them ate meat, whereas others ate plants. One group of plant eaters became very much like mammals. But the ancestry of mammals and humans is found in the small meat-eating cynodonts.

Swift and deadly dinosaurs came to dominate the land during the Triassic period. Most of the cynodonts were killed off. Only those most successful at hiding survived. Besides gradually becoming smaller and therefore harder to notice, cynodonts grew used to living at night. These tiny nocturnal survivors became mammals.

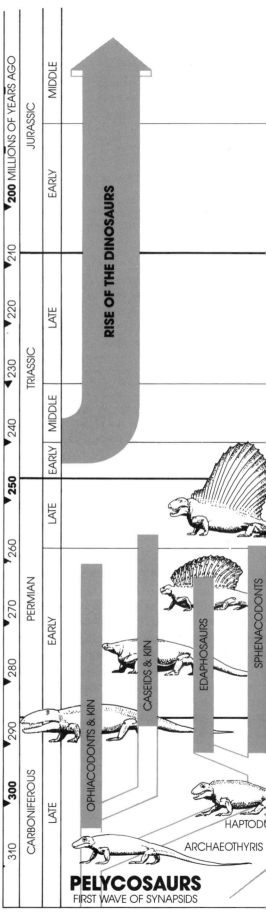

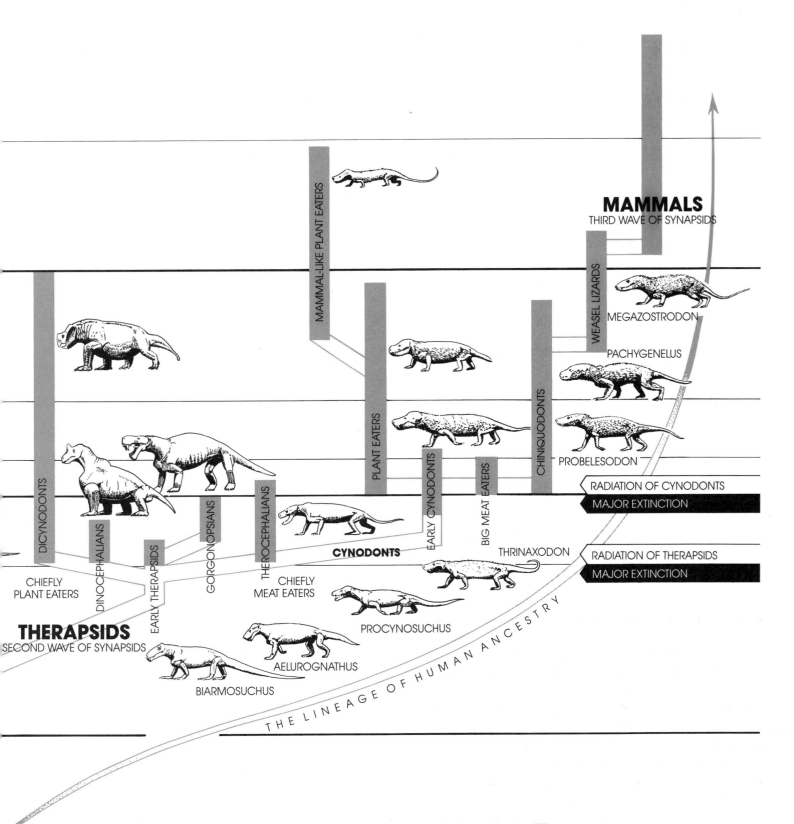

MAMMAL-LIKE PLANT EATERS

MAMMALS
THIRD WAVE OF SYNAPSIDS

WEASEL LIZARDS

MEGAZOSTRODON

PACHYGENELUS

PLANT EATERS

CHINIQUODONTS

PROBELESODON

DICYNODONTS

GORGONOPSIANS

THEROCEPHALIANS

EARLY CYNODONTS

BIG MEAT EATERS

RADIATION OF CYNODONTS

MAJOR EXTINCTION

DINOCEPHALIANS

EARLY THERAPSIDS

CYNODONTS

THRINAXODON

RADIATION OF THERAPSIDS

MAJOR EXTINCTION

CHIEFLY
PLANT EATERS

CHIEFLY
MEAT EATERS

PROCYNOSUCHUS

THERAPSIDS
SECOND WAVE OF SYNAPSIDS

AELUROGNATHUS

BIARMOSUCHUS

THE LINEAGE OF HUMAN ANCESTRY

The Synapsid Family Tree

THE FIRST REPTILES

Haptodus—came with its own set of steak knives.

HAPTODUS
EARLY PERMIAN
ACTUAL SIZE
FOR A SKELETAL VIEW, SEE PAGE 116.

The sphenacodonts were the meat-eating pelycosaurs. Their most famous member was the spectacular finback *Dimetrodon*, the largest predator of its day. Less spectacular both in size and appearance, was *Haptodus* (HAP-tuh-dus), named for its "fastened teeth." It is through this comparatively ordinary reptile that we continue our journey through human ancestry.

Happy had a perpetual grin. It was formed by the natural curve of the jawline, even deeper than that of *Archaeothyris* (see pages 60 and 61). Happy also had larger, sharper, narrow-bladed, knifelike teeth, ideal for slicing through meat.

Different-sized teeth were put to different uses. The largest teeth, set in the middle of Happy's jaw, punctured the scaly skin of its victims. Happy's front teeth were shorter to nip bits of flesh from bone. The back teeth were small to chop large pieces into small ones that could be swallowed. This is close to the pattern of mammal and human teeth.

Happy was among the first reptiles that chopped some of its food to pieces. Smaller pieces digest more quickly and release their energy more quickly. This enables an animal to become more active, which helps in obtaining more food.

As a predator, Happy had to be faster than its prey. Happy's limbs were long and slender compared with those of other pelycosaurs. We know from living animals, such as dogs, that long

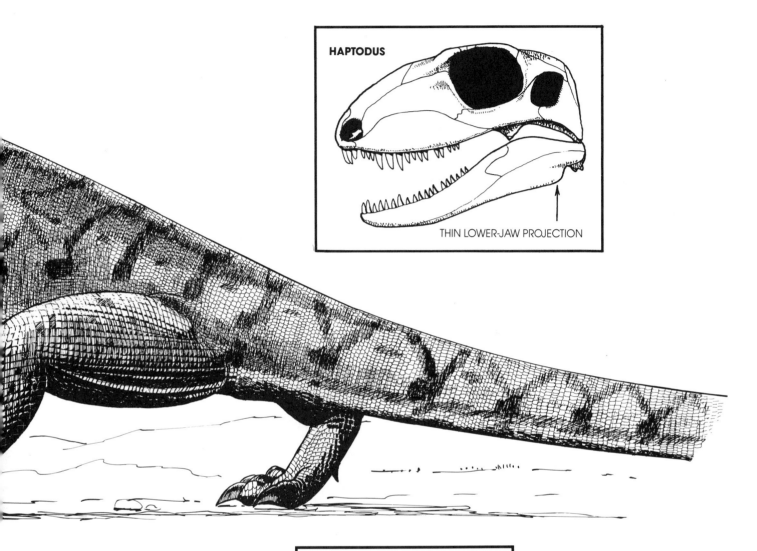

HAPTODUS

THIN LOWER-JAW PROJECTION

What's New?

Larger knifelike teeth
Limbs longer, more slender
Stronger back
Three ribs attach to pelvis
Jaws with narrow rear projection

slender limbs usually give animals greater speed.

Three pairs of Happy's ribs connected to its pelvis. This provided added strength to keep the body off the ground. Greater support also came from elongated spines along the backbone. Each one was an important anchor for strong back muscles and ligaments.

One minor detail of Happy's anatomy deserves special attention because of its later importance.

Happy's lower jaw had a thin portion projecting off the bottom toward the rear. About 60 million years later it

would frame a descendant's eardrum. When resting its jaws on the ground, Happy would have sensed nearby footsteps because this thinner bone would have been sensitive to ground vibrations (see page 56).

Happy ranged in size from 2 to 4½ feet in length. During the early Permian period, 280 million years ago, Happy lived on dry floodplains in Europe and in the American Southwest. At that time both areas were part of one large equatorial continent.

Biarmosuchus—an early-morning jogger.

Most reptiles live in the tropics, where temperatures and seasons are more or less constant. In contrast, many therapsids (see pages 62-63) lived near the poles. One of the most primitive of these was *Biarmosuchus* (bi-arm-uh-SOOK-us), or "two-shouldered crocodile"

Bee stood with arms and thighs extended downward at an angle, not straight out to the sides, as in *Haptodus* (see page 64). Bee's shoulder blades were less bulky and rode more loosely on the rib cage. By moving, they helped to lengthen each stride.

Although Bee had the same number of joints in each digit, Bee's outer four "fingers" and toes were more equal in length. This indicates that Bee was swinging its feet directly beneath its wrists and ankles during the cycle of each stride, rather than out to the side. Longer toes would have dragged. Toes were shortened by reducing some of the finger bones to mere disks.

Bee depended more on its swinging legs and less on its swinging backbone to get around. This helped Bee breathe. Until this development, ancestors had had to hold their breath while moving at full speed. While their backbones were swinging from side to side, they could not have expanded both sides of their rib cages at the same time to inhale. One side of ribs always contracted as the other expanded. By undulating its back less, Bee was able to expand both sides of its rib cage at the same time, even at full speed. With this advantage, Bee could cover longer distances without growing tired. Increased stamina was helpful in hunting for and running down prey.

Muscle activity creates heat that can be used to warm up a chilly reptile. Bee's new stance may have

BIARMOSUCHUS
LATE PERMIAN
LESS THAN ONE-THIRD ACTUAL SIZE
FOR A SKELETAL VIEW, SEE PAGE 116.

signaled the beginning of an endothermic ("internally warmed") body. Instead of waiting for the sun's warmth, Bee might have shivered, vibrating its muscles to generate heat.

To produce more heat, the body needs more food as fuel. This predator was well equipped to deal with large prey. Huge canine teeth, typical of the therapsids, jutted like sabers from the upper jaws. Bee's snout was longer and its jaw was better leveraged, making each bite more powerful.

What's New?

Larger canines
Jawbone better leveraged
Larger, thinner projection on lower edge of lower jaws
Limbs angled downward, knees forward, elbows back
Floating shoulder girdle
Digits more equal in size
Range extended beyond the tropics
Possibly endothermic

Bee's third eye was larger than it ever had been in previous ancestors, and it was raised on a bump of bone.

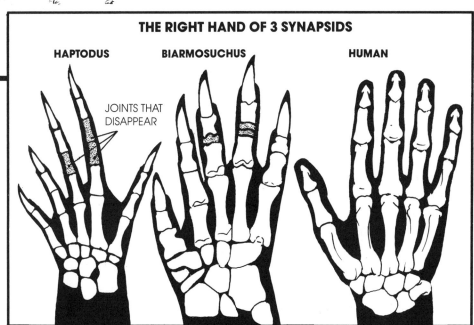

THE RIGHT HAND OF 3 SYNAPSIDS

HAPTODUS   BIARMOSUCHUS   HUMAN

JOINTS THAT
DISAPPEAR

As in the first fish (see pages 38-39), this third eye controlled hormones connected to reproduction. With more extreme seasonal changes to contend with, the breeding cycle had to be more accurately timed by the secretions emitted from this eye/gland.

Bee lived at the start of the late Permian period, 258 million years ago, on floodplains now uplifted by the Ural mountains in the Soviet Union. At that time, as today, that area was not far from the Arctic Circle.

Aelurognathus—its skull began to open up.

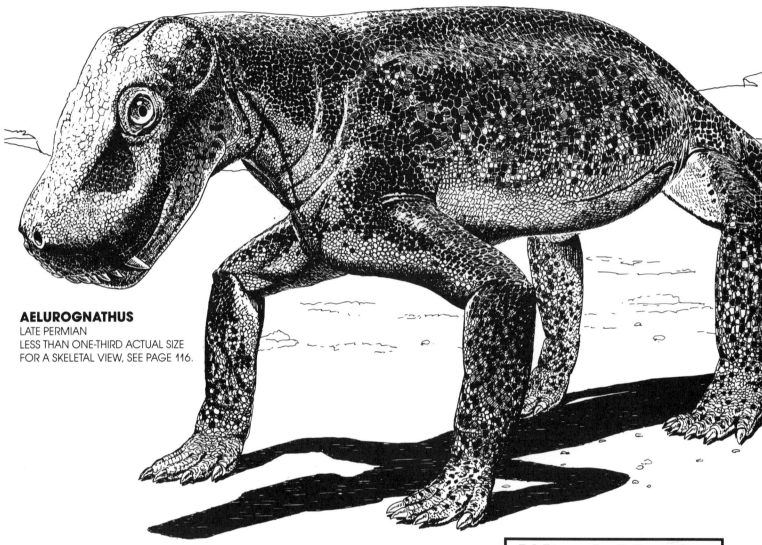

AELUROGNATHUS
LATE PERMIAN
LESS THAN ONE-THIRD ACTUAL SIZE
FOR A SKELETAL VIEW, SEE PAGE 116.

What's New?

Enlarged synapsid skull openings
Wider, flatter head
Larger jaw muscles
Third eye smaller
Backbone stronger
Tail shorter
Large lower canines

Reptiles have jaw muscles inside their skulls. Mammals have jaw muscles outside their skulls. In *Aelurognathus* (ee-lur-OG-nuh-thus), or "cat jaw," the change from one to the other was just beginning.

Like primitive fish (see page 40), a reptile has an internal braincase within its boxy outer skull. Jaw muscles fill the space between the two. A mammal, on the other hand, has lost most of its boxy outer skull. Only jaw muscles and skin cover the braincase. All that remains of the outer reptilian skull in mammals is the slender cheekbone and the bones of the face.

In Aely's case, the skull openings at the temples were growing large and close together (illustrated on page 69). The edges of these openings became new attachment points for even bigger jaw muscles. As these enlarged, the back of Aely's head became broader.

Aely's giant jaw muscles were attached to a large elevated area on the one jawbone that had teeth growing from it (illustrated on pages 120-121). This area, called the coro-

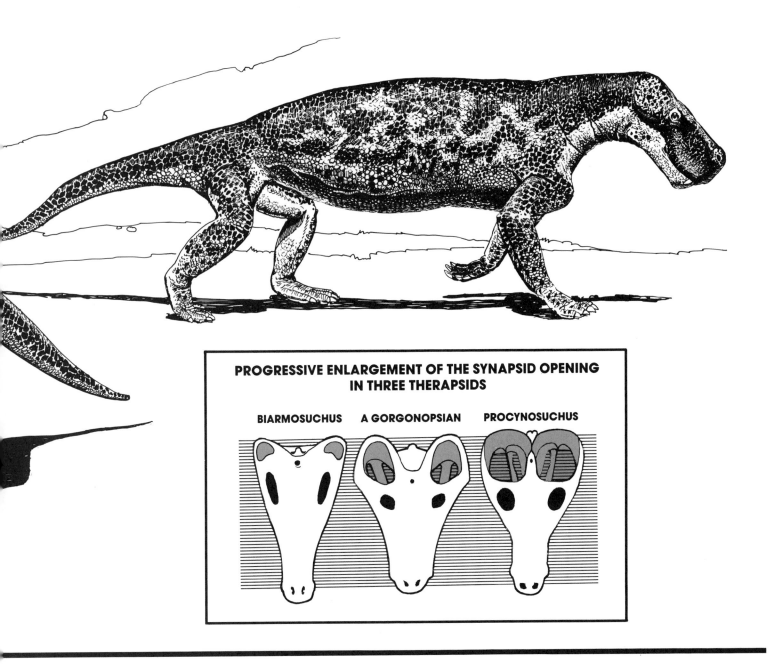

PROGRESSIVE ENLARGEMENT OF THE SYNAPSID OPENING IN THREE THERAPSIDS

BIARMOSUCHUS   A GORGONOPSIAN   PROCYNOSUCHUS

noid process, makes up most of the back half of the human jaw. This is the part that rises above the line of teeth at the rear. It provides a lever to produce a strong bite even when the jaws are wide open.

With the tooth-bearing jaw element becoming more important, the other jawbones at the back became less important for feeding. They loosened up, and in doing so, probably became better at conducting sound vibrations.

Aely had a shorter tail. This meant that its sturdy backbone was taking on more load-lifting duties. Muscles that connected leg bones to tail bones were shifting, becoming rump muscles. The counterbalancing effect of a long heavy tail was no longer needed. Dinosaurs used their long tails as a counterbalance. A short tail meant that synapsid reptiles could not rise up on their hind feet alone.

Aely was a gorgonopsian. Gorgonopsians were named for the mythological snake-headed witches known as gorgons, one of whom was Medusa. In addition to their upper fangs, gorgonopsians also grew large lower canines.

Aely lived in the late Permian period, 250 million years ago, in South Africa. At that time the area was a near-polar region of a supercontinent where there may have been snowfall.

Procynosuchus—the cheeky chewer.

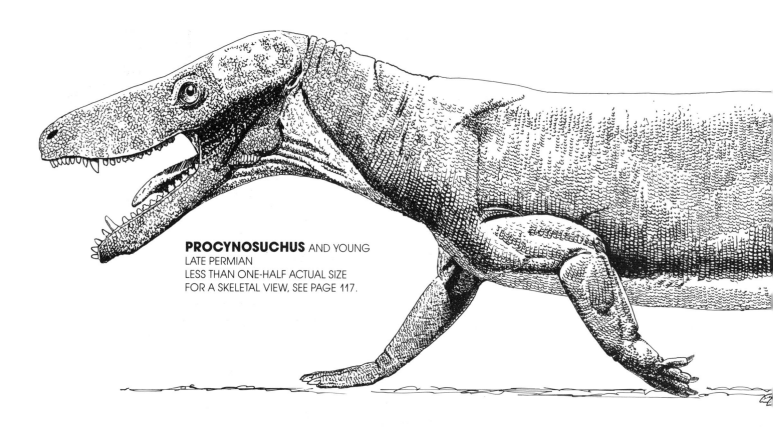

PROCYNOSUCHUS AND YOUNG
LATE PERMIAN
LESS THAN ONE-HALF ACTUAL SIZE
FOR A SKELETAL VIEW, SEE PAGE 117.

The changeover from reptile to mammal sped up 250 million years ago when the first of the cynodonts (see pages 62-63) appeared. It concluded some 40 million years later with the origin of true mammals.

Cynodonts are known by their widely flaring cheekbones, huge synapsid skull openings, multi-pointed cheek teeth, a new shelf of bone separating their nasal cavity from their mouth, and other mammal-like features.

The 40-inch-long *Procynosuchus* (pro-sine-oh-SOOK-us), or "before the dog-crocodile," is one of the earliest known cynodonts. Pro chewed its food. Chewing breaks down food even faster than chopping does. It results in even quicker digestion and the faster release of a meal's energy. Because

Pro's upper teeth slid snugly past the lower teeth, this cynodont was able to shred its food to pieces but not grind it to a pulp.

Pro's broad cheekbones served as places to attach new jaw muscles. You feel similar muscles below your cheekbone whenever you clench your jaws. They line up your molars when you chew.

Pro's chewing teeth had multiple points, unlike ordinary reptile teeth. More points kept the teeth from sinking in too deeply. Instead, they shredded meat apart with every bite.

Lungfish, amphibians, and living reptiles have a low metabolism and go through long periods of time without breathing. Unlike them, Pro had a higher metabolism and had to breathe more regularly, even while chewing.

What's New?

Widely flaring cheekbones framing large synapsid openings
Multi-pointed cheek teeth
Secondary palate
Head-to-neck ball joint splits in two
Ribs shorten and straighten in lower back
A fourth rib connects to pelvis
Pelvis holes appear below the leg socket
Palate teeth disappear

A new shelf of bone separating Pro's nasal cavity from the rest of its mouth, called the secondary palate, helped it keep breathing. This new palate changed the path of incoming air from just behind the front teeth to the back of the throat. (See illustration above.) This shelf also strengthened the skull and was a platform against

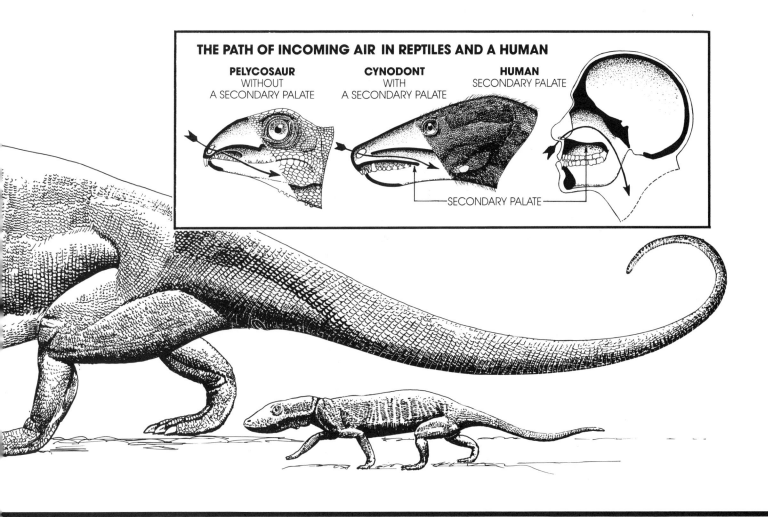

THE PATH OF INCOMING AIR IN REPTILES AND A HUMAN

PELYCOSAUR
WITHOUT
A SECONDARY PALATE

CYNODONT
WITH
A SECONDARY PALATE

HUMAN
SECONDARY PALATE

SECONDARY PALATE

which the tongue could move food around for more effective chewing. Your tongue is probably touching your secondary palate right now.

Palate teeth near the throat disappeared because Pro was no longer bolting down live prey. It killed first, then ate.

In most reptiles and birds, a single ball-and-socket joint attaches the skull to the neck, like a trailer hitch. This type is the strongest of all and can move in any direction. It has one drawback. Whenever the neck bends forward, the sensitive spinal cord resting just above this joint is stretched. And when the neck bends back, the spinal cord becomes compressed. In Pro's case, the ball joint connecting the head to the neck began dividing in two. In mammals, twin ball joints line

up on either side of the spinal-cord opening. In this way the cord is neither compressed nor stretched when the head nods yes, but it prevents the head from moving to the left and right. Twin trailer hitches don't allow rotation. That motion was allowed by the next joint in the neck.

Ribs in the lower part of Pro's back (the lumbar region) were short and straight, as in humans. Fossils show that this area was relatively stiff. Here is another clue that cynodonts were shifting away from the undulating backbone style of walking.

Four ribs connected to Pro's pelvis for greater support. A pair of large holes appeared in the lower portion of the pelvis, below the leg socket. These new pelvic holes were areas for stronger inner-thigh-muscle attach-

ments. These holes are to be found in all cynodonts, mammals, and humans.

Some animals keep, as adults, certain features of their youth. This has happened many times in the ancestry of humans. A Pro hatchling closely resembled full-sized early mammals (see page 78). It had a head and braincase of a similar size and also a slender cheekbone. Both Pro hatchlings and adult early mammals lacked a bony strut behind their eyeballs. Unlike baby mammals, however, these baby cynodonts had a full set of sharp teeth. Evidently they were fully able to fend for themselves shortly after hatching.

Pro was a contemporary of *Aelurognathus* (see page 68). Both lived in South Africa during the late Permian period, 250 million years ago.

Thrinaxodon—was it hairy and scaly?

THRINAXODON
EARLY TRIASSIC
ACTUAL SIZE
FOR A SKELETAL VIEW, SEE PAGE 117.

Among the early survivors of the Permian/Triassic extinction event was a cynodont known as *Thrinaxodon* (thrin-AKS-uh-don). It was a long-bodied predator named for its "trident-shaped teeth."

It seems that all adult therapsids were able to create at least some of their own body heat. Cynodonts were probably better at it than others. The best proof of this comes from ridges in Thriny's nose that probably supported tiny bones called nasal scrolls. In living mammals, nasal scrolls disrupt the flow of air in each breath. Disrupted air is warmed and humidified before it enters the lungs. On the way out,

moisture from each hot breath condenses on these cooler scrolls. This works the way warm air condenses on a glass filled with an ice-cold drink. That is why your dog's nose is always cool and wet (if it's healthy!).

Making heat was one thing, but staying warm was another matter. Bulky bodies help larger endotherms stay warm. Smaller ones need some other form of insulation. Fatty tissues help. So does hair. Even a few dozen strands per square inch are enough to break up the flow of air near the body, trapping it as dead air. Dead air trapped between the fluffed-up feathers of a down jacket is what insulates

What's New?

Pineal eye/gland disappears from surface
Complete secondary palate
Nasal scrolls
Mammalian number of teeth
Three-cusped cheek teeth with staggered placement
More nearly erect hind limbs
Shorter, thinner tail
Larger synapsid opening
Five ribs connect to pelvis
Broad plates on ribs
Probable: Hair

the wearer against the cold.

Like scales and fingernails, hair is also made of keratin. It grows from the outer skin layer. In mammals with scaly tails, such as opossums, hair

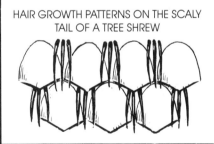

HAIR GROWTH PATTERNS ON THE SCALY
TAIL OF A TREE SHREW

grows at the joints between scales. Most other mammals grow hair in patterns as if scales were still present. Look at the back of your hand and you'll see that humans do, too.

Thriny probably had soft tiny scales with hairs growing between them. Cynodonts produced two great clans, one of plant eaters and one of meat eaters. Both clans produced many tiny endotherms (see pages 62 and 63). We know that the tiny meat eaters were hairy because their

descendants, tiny primitive mammals (such as shrews), have dense hair. Hair is the most likely insulator for the tiniest of the plant-eating clan as well. If hair did not evolve independently in each of the two groups, then both probably inherited this trait from their last common ancestor, *Thrinaxodon.*

Thriny had roughly the same number of teeth as a primitive mammal. They were also similar in shape. The cheek teeth, for instance, had a number of cusps, or points, all in a row.

Following a trend begun by the first therapsids, Thriny had a stiff back. Its ribs had large overlapping plates, making the trunk more rigid.

(For an interesting comparison, see *Ichthyostega*, pages 50-51.)

Thriny's hind limbs were held closer to its body than in previous ancestors. With reduced strain, the muscles needed to hold them up were smaller. The shape of the pelvis reflected this change in posture. Thriny's elbows, in contrast, remained well out to the sides.

Thriny lived during the early Triassic period, 242 million years ago. This cynodont ranged across Antarctica and the southernmost portions of Africa. At that time both areas were parts of one continent and lay just north of the Antarctic Circle.

Probelesodon—with a little spring in its step.

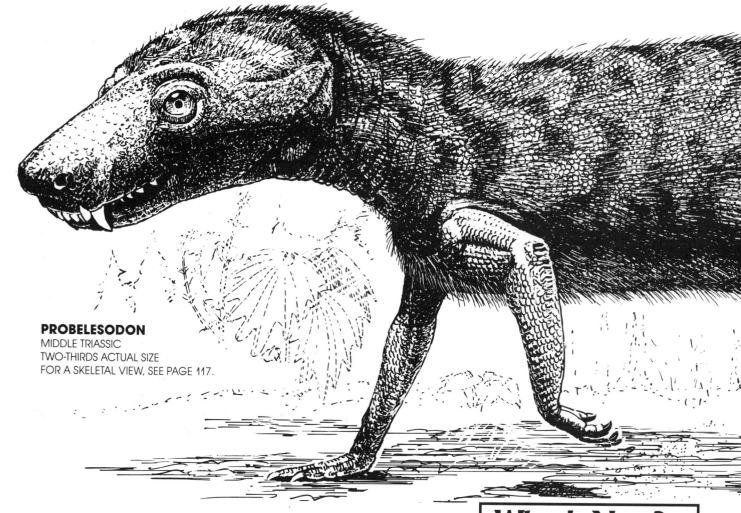

PROBELESODON
MIDDLE TRIASSIC
TWO-THIRDS ACTUAL SIZE
FOR A SKELETAL VIEW, SEE PAGE 117.

Cynodonts more advanced than *Thrinaxodon* (see page 72) come in three basic varieties: plant eaters, large meat eaters, and small meat eaters. Small meat eaters are known as chiniquodonts (chin-eh-KWOE-donts), or "Chiniquá (Brazil) tooth."

Probelesodon (pro-bel-EES-uh-don), or "before dart tooth," was a chiniquodont cynodont the size of a small dog. Proby's skull openings took up more than half of the skull surface. They must have housed very powerful jaw muscles. Major portions of the braincase had turned from cartilage to bone. Bone provided a stronger base of origin for the powerful jaw muscles.

A new projection from Proby's greatly enlarged tooth-bearing bone extended backward (illustrated on pages 120-121). It supported the much smaller jawbones behind it still acting as the jaw joint. In so doing, this projection nearly touched the skull side by side with that joint. In mammals, this new projection indeed is the skull/jaw joint and the smaller jawbones dwindle in size. In Proby's case, they had become almost useless for eating but better at conducting sound vibrations.

There is a groove at the back of cynodont cheekbones. This may have held an ear canal leading from a sur-

What's New?

Enlarged synapsid openings
Braincase turns from cartilage to bone
Jawbone more mammal-like
Larger head
Ear canal leading to eardrum
Not so long-waisted
Ribs modern in appearance
Legs longer and more slender
Longer heels on feet, plus Achilles tendon

face hole to an inner eardrum, the same as in humans. Sound came through this hole and also along the jaws. Not enough has been learned about cynodont ears to know how

well these animals heard. It was probably not as well as living lizards hear.

Proby's head was large in proportion to its body. The brain, however, remained quite small. Proby was not so long-waisted as its ancestor had been. The ribs were modern in appearance. That meant the torso muscles and backbone had taken over the supporting duty the expanded ribs of *Thrinaxodon* once held.

Proby had longer, more slender legs than did earlier cynodonts. The hind feet had extensions of bone out the rear of each foot, called heels. They formed attachment points for the Achilles tendons. In humans, kan-

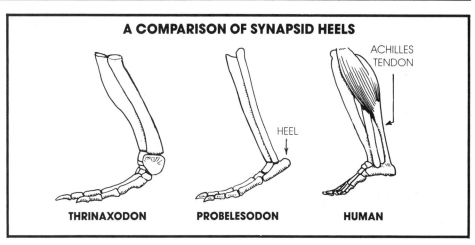

A COMPARISON OF SYNAPSID HEELS

ACHILLES TENDON

HEEL

THRINAXODON   **PROBELESODON**   **HUMAN**

garoos, and other mammals, this tendon provides spring to each step. After it is stretched out, it rebounds like a rubber band, making walking easier.

Proby lived during the middle Triassic period, 235 million years ago, in temperate southern South America, still part of a supercontinent.

Pachygenelus—the little runt with supertough teeth.

About the size of a hamster, *Pachygenelus* (pak-ee-JEN-eh-lus) was named for its "thick little chin." It was one of the last group of meat-eating cynodonts, the "weasel lizards." This group is known only from tiny fragmentary remains. Nevertheless, we do know they were the closest cousins of mammals.

With the widespread appearance of the swift and deadly dinosaurs some 220 million years ago, cynodonts larger than a rabbit didn't stand a chance. Only those that were tiny or hidden out of sight survived. Runts had a better chance of surviving. They also had the ability to produce smaller eggs that hatched prematurely.

The smaller an internally warmed animal is, the more heat it loses to the air. Because of its small adult size, Paky was probably insulated with a dense coat of fur, like a living mouse or shrew.

After making a nest, the female "weasel lizard" probably lost hair on her belly. In the same way, some birds lose feathers on their brood patches before laying eggs. Skin-to-skin contact directs body heat more efficiently to eggs and hatchlings. Unlike their parents, the babies of tiny mammals are not warm-blooded and they have a low metabolism. They are hairless, so they may receive heat from their mother's body directly.

In the absence of milk, baby food must have been vomited into the nest by the mother. This is how bird nestlings and wolf pups receive their food.

These tiny, naked, and perhaps toothless hatchlings could survive only with their mother's care. Without having to keep themselves warm, or feed themselves, "weasel lizard" babies could devote all their energies to maturing quickly.

PACHYGENELUS AND EGGS
EARLY JURASSIC
ACTUAL SIZE

Another reason why the "weasel lizards" did not grow very large is that their bone-growth patterns had changed. As all vertebrates grow, they replace flexible cartilage with stiff and sturdy bone. In typical reptile leg bones, this process begins in the middle of each shaft and proceeds to either end. The cartilage would be completely replaced in short order except for the fact that more cartilage keeps growing at the ends, which makes the reptile grow larger and larger. That is why the oldest crocodiles are also the biggest. In most mammals, bone also grows from the joints back toward the middle. Cartilage is restricted to narrow bands between the bony portions, and this is where growth occurs. Once these bands become completely replaced by bone, growth stops. That is why human growth stops during or shortly after the teenage years.

What's New?

Smaller overall size
Changing bone-growth patterns
Eye-socket-bone brace disappears
Cheekbones thinner
Cheek teeth wider, with grooved
 roots
Crystalline enamel coating on teeth
Probable:
 Diet of insects and worms
 Dense fur
 Hairless immature hatchlings
 Parental nesting care
 Scales disappear, except on tail

As in most mammals, there was no bar of bone separating Paky's eye sockets from its synapsid skull openings. In other words, Paky's eyeball and jaw muscle occupied the same space just above the slender cheekbone. The ring of bone inside the eyeball itself was probably lost at about this time, too. No mammals have such a ring.

Paky's teeth were much wider than those of typical cynodonts. They chopped food better. The roots of the cheek teeth (molars) were wide, with a groove running down the middle. In

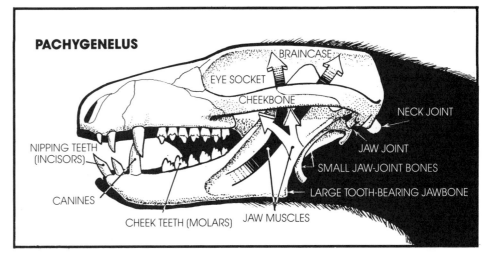

BONE-GROWTH PATTERNS

CARTILAGE
BONE
CARTILAGE

REPTILE BONE
Growth from center to both ends

CARTILAGE
BONE
CARTILAGE
BONE
CARTILAGE
BONE
CARTILAGE

MAMMAL BONE
Growth from center <u>and</u> at either end

PACHYGENELUS

BRAINCASE
EYE SOCKET
CHEEKBONE
NECK JOINT
JAW JOINT
SMALL JAW-JOINT BONES
LARGE TOOTH-BEARING JAWBONE
NIPPING TEETH (INCISORS)
CANINES
CHEEK TEETH (MOLARS)
JAW MUSCLES

mammal molars, this groove actually divides the root in two for a sturdier attachment.

Paky's teeth were extra tough. The enamel had a crystalline structure that made each tooth coating nearly as strong as steel but not so brittle. Many mammals have this same kind of tooth enamel. Stronger teeth are important to mammals because they have only two sets in their lifetime, the milk teeth and the permanent teeth. Like most reptiles, Paky continued to shed its teeth throughout its lifetime but evidently at a much slower rate than was typical.

Because of its size, Paky probably ate insects and worms.

Paky lived during the early Jurassic period, 205 million years ago, in tropical to subtropical South Africa and Nova Scotia (Canada). At that time these were both parts of the same supercontinent.

WEASEL LIZARDS HAD TO HIDE TO AVOID BEING EATEN BY EARLY DINOSAURS

Megazostrodon—a reptilelike mammal with milk glands.

Mammal mothers feed their young milk produced in milk glands. Glands are soft tissues that do not become fossils. The earliest known mammal that had milk glands is *Megazostrodon* (meg-uh-ZOS-troe-don), named for its "big girdled teeth." The reason why Mega's teeth tell scientists that it had milk glands takes a little explanation.

Reptiles shed their teeth continually. Each new tooth is larger than the one before it as long as the reptile keeps growing. A minor drawback to shedding teeth is that there are gaps in each tooth row. This is really no problem when all of the teeth are nearly identical. Simple biting continues.

A mammal's molars, on the other hand, are specially shaped. There must always be opposite partners to slice or mash against. This is why molars are permanent in mammals and the milk or first set of teeth are replaced only once.

In mammals, the baby or milk teeth develop so chewing can begin. These do not appear until the jaws are large enough to hold them. When the jaws grow larger, the milk teeth are pushed out by the larger permanent teeth.

Newborn mammals are born toothless because their jaws are too small to hold teeth and they don't need them. They depend on milk from their mother's milk glands for nourishment.

Mega had both molars and premolars. Only mammals have such teeth, so scientists assume it followed the typical mammalian pattern. Upon hatching, it would have been toothless and therefore would have found nourishment only at its mother's milk glands.

Primitive egg-laying mammals,

MEGAZOSTRODON
EARLY JURASSIC
ACTUAL SIZE
FOR A SKELETAL VIEW,
SEE PAGE 118.

MORGANUCODON

EGG & HATCHLING
ACTUAL SIZE

HATCHLING 5x ACTUAL SIZE

What's New?

Molars and premolars (single tooth-replacement pattern)
Mammalian type jaw hinge
Neck and tail ribs reduced or fused to vertebrae
More flexible backbone
Smaller overall size
Much larger brain
Nasal openings merge
Probable:
  Breast milk
  New skin glands
  New nerve endings
  Large intestine (colon)
  Loss of most color vision
  Increased sensitivity to dim light
  Primitive penis

such as echidnas and the platypus, have milk glands that may have been similar to those of early mammals.

The platypus secretes fluids from skin glands in order to maintain the suppleness of its fur. These fluids are rich in fats, salts, and nutrients. Platypus milk glands, on the other hand, produce a slightly different fluid containing oily fats and proteins. This milk lacks only the sugars that most mammal's milk has.

Platypus milk comes from glands called milk lines that run along the adult female's abdomen. In other mammals, milk glands may appear anywhere along these lines, according to species (see Mammal Breasts illustration). Like living egg-laying mammals, Mega had no teats, or nipples. Milk oozed from milk lines and collected in a puddle on the belly. Babies had to suck

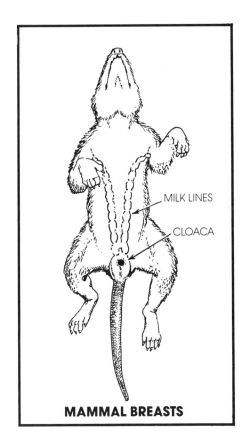

MAMMAL BREASTS

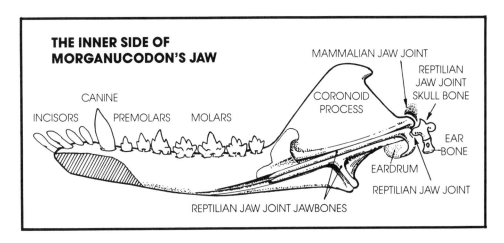

their milk from this puddle the best they could.

Mega had a mammalian jaw joint (illustrated on pages 120-121). The tooth-bearing bone formed a new jaw joint alongside the other one. Both continued working together, although the former jaw-joint bones became looser and smaller, better able to pick up higher-pitched sound vibrations.

Early mammals may have been active only after dark. In that way they avoided the dinosaurs that wanted to eat them and the sunlight that might have overheated them.

Overheating is very dangerous for mammals. Very few can run a high fever without lethal results. Mammals unload heat by sweating, panting, and redirecting blood flow to the thinner and naked parts of their anatomy such as the nostrils, mouth, ears, legs, and tail, where air cools it.

In order to avoid spending energy and water trying to cool off, a mammal's body temperature is set slightly higher than the highest outdoor temperature it is likely to encounter regularly in nature. Humans and other daylight animals have a temperature of 98.6 degrees Fahrenheit because daytime temperatures rarely get hotter than that. Mammals that are active at night deal with cooler and more constant temperatures. Everywhere they go is in the shade. Their body temperatures and metabolism are set at a lower level than those of daylight mammals. Their food requirements are lower as well.

Mega must have had a low metabolism (see page 38) and also a low body temperature. Perhaps it was 15 degrees cooler than that of a typical daylight-living mammal, such as a human. So, this mammal was not exactly "warm-blooded." But it was able to create its own heat and keep its internal temperature fairly constant.

When the weather is cold, most mammals hibernate. They sleep and their metabolism lowers. They live off food stored in their body fat.

Mega's sensory system improved as this midnight rambler scrambled in the dark through the forest litter of the Jurassic period.

Nerves that register warmth, cold, touch, and pressure are much more plentiful in the skin of mammals than in reptiles. While reptiles have taste buds all over their mouth, taste buds are concentrated on the tongue of mammals.

Mega's eyes became more sensitive to lower light levels at the expense of losing sensitivity to color. Today, most mammals cannot see many colors. Primates, including humans, are an exception.

As a nighttime predator, Mega came to rely on senses other than sight to find prey and avoid enemies. Typically, Mega had to follow trails by relying on odors. Smell is of little importance to humans, but in most reptiles and especially in mammals it is a major source of information.

Morganucodon (more-gan-OOK-uh-don), named for a small town in Wales, was another early mammal from the same time period whose skull is better known than Mega's.

Morgan's nasal openings merged to form one large hole at the tip of the skull (as in modern mammals and humans). On the skin surface, however, two fleshy nostril openings

Megazostrodon—continued.

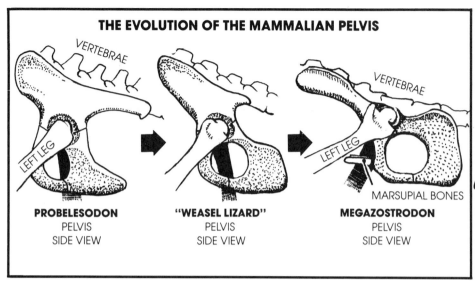

THE EVOLUTION OF THE MAMMALIAN PELVIS

VERTEBRAE

LEFT LEG

PROBELESODON
PELVIS
SIDE VIEW

VERTEBRAE

LEFT LEG

"WEASEL LIZARD"
PELVIS
SIDE VIEW

VERTEBRAE

LEFT LEG

MARSUPIAL BONES

MEGAZOSTRODON
PELVIS
SIDE VIEW

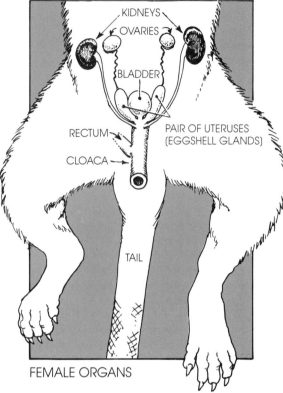

KIDNEYS

OVARIES

BLADDER

RECTUM

PAIR OF UTERUSES
(EGGSHELL GLANDS)

CLOACA

TAIL

FEMALE ORGANS

remained. The part of Morgan's brain devoted to smelling was greatly enlarged. This must have meant a greater ability to detect odors and tell them apart.

Morgan had better hearing than any cynodont. The inner-ear casing below the brain was so large, it became the biggest feature there.

In the dark, information about their world did not come easily for Morgan and Mega. Their brain had to decipher every shadow, every sound, and every odor. Early mammals had to imagine the world as if they could see it. In humans, powerful images and emotions still arise from certain scents and sounds. Along with imagination came dreams. Mammal brains keep forming images even while the rest of the body sleeps.

Morgan had a brain that was several times larger than that of an advanced cynodont of similar overall size. It wasn't just a larger brain, it was a different kind of brain. It had new lobes of gray matter that developed from the smell centers. Within these new lobes, memory, association, and learning could all take place. Many of the sen-

sory nerves went there, as well. With their tiny brains, cynodonts relied only on instinct for survival. Morgan's brain had the ability to reprogram itself as it learned how to deal with new situations in new ways. Morgan could be taught by following its mother.

Mega's limbs show a greater range of motion. The knees tucked in close to the body, but the elbows did not. That is because the pelvis became entirely mammalian (see illustration above) while the simple shoulder bones remained basically like those of cynodonts. In mammals, the pelvic plate above each leg socket is a slender bar that sticks out only in front. Frogs have a similar pelvis. Like frogs, small mammals keep their hind legs bent in a permanent crouch, ready to spring at prey or away from foes. Mongooses and polecats can dodge the strikes of poisonous snakes because they are always ready to jump.

Because of the nature of their interlocking vertebrae, birds and reptiles do not lie on their sides. In Mega's case, the backbone could twist, allowing this mammal to lie on its side.

With this adaptation, grooming and attending nursing young became easier.

Mammals have an addition to their intestines known as the colon or large intestine. Bacteria collect there to break down tough plant fibers mammals themselves cannot digest. Before undigestable waste exits the body, most of its water is reabsorbed by the colon.

Female *Megazostrodons* had genitals similar to those of living egg-laying mammals. Like its walking fish ancestors, Mega had a cloaca, a single tube into which digestive waste, urine, and eggs all passed through on their way to the outside. At the deepest end of the cloaca were a pair of uteruses. In most animals, the uterus is the organ that nourishes eggs and produces a secretion that hardens to form a shell around each one.

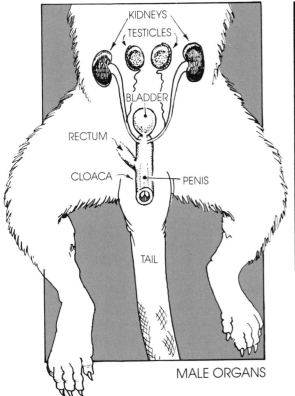

MALE ORGANS

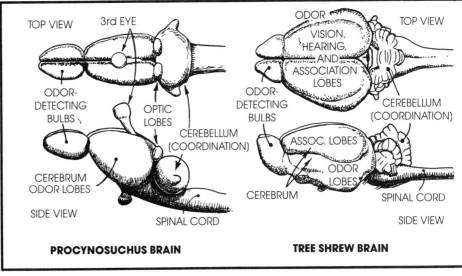

PROCYNOSUCHUS BRAIN

TREE SHREW BRAIN

THE EVOLUTION OF A LOWER MOLAR

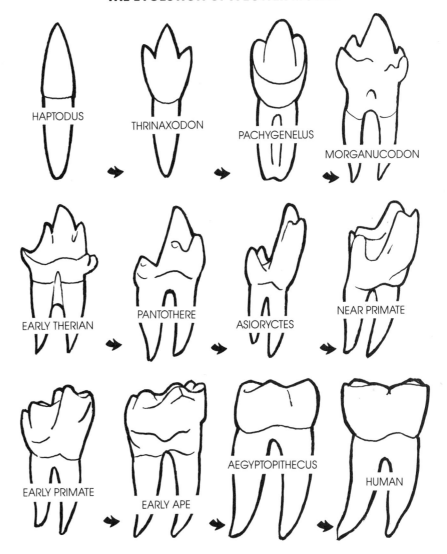

Male *Megazostrodons* also had a cloaca to shuttle digestive waste and urine to the outside. Males also had a penis, which some unknown synapsid had acquired sometime previously. In the males of egg-laying mammals, the penis is usually kept sheathed beneath the surface within the cloaca. During mating, however, it is extended outside of the body and inserted into the female's cloaca to conduct sperm fluid to her eggs. Urine was not conducted through the penis at this stage. The testicles did not descend outside the body.

Mega lived during the earliest part of the Jurassic period, 210 million years ago in southern Africa. At the same time in the temperate Northern Hemisphere, Morgan lived in what is now England and China. At that time, all these areas were temperate and parts of the same vast supercontinent.

The Mammal Family Tree—a dynasty with humble beginning

The chart to the right is an overview of the family tree of mammals from 220 million years ago to the present. The history of the mammals can be divided roughly into thirds.

During the entire Jurassic period, mammals remained small and secretive, perhaps entirely nocturnal. They were beady-eyed, egg-laying furballs that nursed their young.

For the duration of the Cretaceous period, a time spanning 80 million years, mammals never grew larger than a house cat. Some began delivering live, but premature, babies. Most gave up sitting on eggs. Cretaceous mammals avoided dinosaurs but were attracted to the flowering trees that were then evolving. Nectar-filled flowers attracted the insects the mammals were eating. Once in the trees, many added fruits, seeds, and bird eggs to their diet.

Following the widespread extinction of the dinosaurs, 65 million years ago, the mammals enjoyed their most recent and grandest third of their long history. Gradually they began appearing in larger and more varied sizes, in the air, on the land, and in the sea. Most of today's mammals had their origins after the dinosaurs became extinct.

Mammals evolved from small meat- and insect-eating cynodonts (see pages 70-77), reptiles with many mammal characteristics. Before long, subtle differences showed up in the shape of mammal molars, indicating that the major groups had split apart.

The most primitive mammals were prototheres ("first-beasts"). Fossils of these ancestors of egg layers are known mostly from their teeth and jaws. Monotremes ("one holed"—referring to the cloaca) are living egg layers. They include two echidnas (or spiny anteaters) and the platypus.

Multituberculates (named for their multi-cusped molars) were the first mammalian plant eaters. They replaced cynodont plant eaters and, in turn, were replaced by rodents, including squirrels, rats, and mice.

Pantotheres ("all beasts") were insect eaters considered to be ancestral to all live-bearing mammals; some say to all living mammals. Only one is known from a complete skeleton (see page 84).

Theria ("beasts") include all mammals with molars having a "reversed triangles" pattern.

Metatheria ("almost beasts") is another name for marsupials (named for their pouch). This group includes both meat-eating and plant-eating forms in a huge variety. The pouch serves as protection for premature babies. Marsupials have only a simple placenta.

Eutheria ("true beasts") have a complex placenta. This organ allows the fetus to develop longer within the mother, often to a fully developed state.

The most primitive of the living eutherians are the insectivores (insect eaters), such as shrews and moles.

Primates are fruit, seed, and insect eaters that took to the trees. They became great climbers. Their close relatives include tree shrews, bats (which can fly), and flying lemurs (which only glide from tree to tree).

Rodents and rabbits are gnawing plant eaters. Their chisel-like front teeth never stop growing but are kept worn down by constant use.

Hoofed mammals began as meat eaters but today include deer, rhino, aardvarks, cattle, and pigs. The ancestors of whales had hooves but went back to the sea, developing flukes and

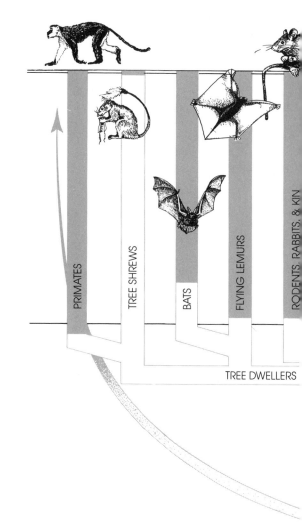

PRIMATES

TREE SHREWS

BATS

FLYING LEMURS

RODENTS, RABBITS, & KIN

TREE DWELLERS

losing their hind limbs in the process. Elephants, sea cows, and their kin are all grazing animals with tusks and flat hooflike nails.

Carnivores have sharp teeth and claws for killing vertebrates.

In contrast, sloths, anteaters, and their kin use their sharp claws to open up termite mounds. A few of these ultimately became plant eaters, but all of them had weak teeth without enamel.

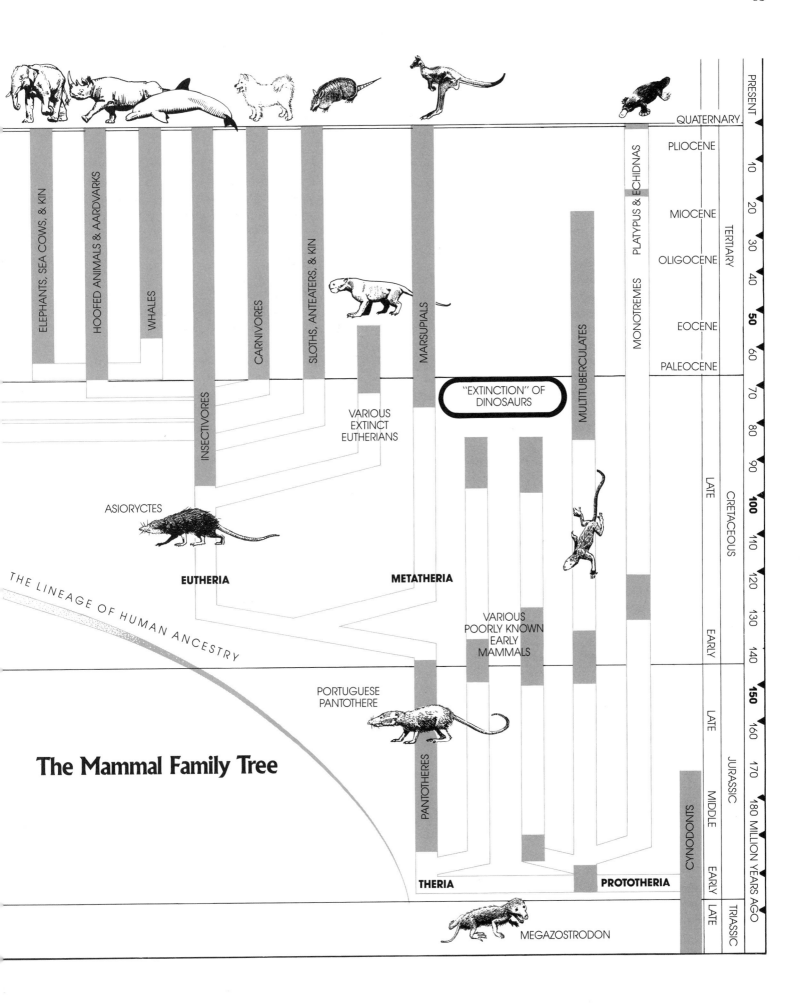

The Mammal Family Tree

THE LINEAGE OF HUMAN ANCESTRY

ELEPHANTS, SEA COWS, & KIN

HOOFED ANIMALS & AARDVARKS

WHALES

CARNIVORES

SLOTHS, ANTEATERS, & KIN

INSECTIVORES

VARIOUS
EXTINCT
EUTHERIANS

ASIORYCTES

EUTHERIA

MARSUPIALS

METATHERIA

"EXTINCTION" OF
DINOSAURS

MULTITUBERCULATES

PLATYPUS & ECHIDNAS

MONOTREMES

VARIOUS
POORLY KNOWN
EARLY
MAMMALS

PORTUGUESE
PANTOTHERE

PANTOTHERES

THERIA

PROTOTHERIA

CYNODONTS

MEGAZOSTRODON

PRESENT

QUATERNARY

PLIOCENE

10

MIOCENE

20

TERTIARY

30

OLIGOCENE

40

50

EOCENE

60

PALEOCENE

70

80

LATE

90

CRETACEOUS

100

110

120

130

EARLY

140

150

LATE

160

JURASSIC

170

MIDDLE

180 MILLION YEARS AGO

EARLY

TRIASSIC

LATE

The Portuguese Pantothere—no eggs, no nest.

The molars of cynodonts and the earliest mammals had three cusps, or points, all in a row. Advanced mammals known as therians, or "beasts," had molars with three cusps arranged in a triangle. The cusp edges sheared past one another in a very precise way, enabling them to slice, crush, and grind a wide variety of food.

Pantotheres, or "all beasts," were among the earliest therians, appearing some 200 million years ago. Most are only known from their teeth and jaws. Some still show traces of tiny reptilian jaw elements attached at the back. Others do not. These tiny bones moved rearward to help conduct and amplify quieter and higher-pitched sounds. One frames the eardrum (see pages 120-121). External earflaps, what we call ears, appeared on the surface to help collect sound waves.

Whiskers are long hairs on the snout and head that act like feelers. They are helpful in getting around in the dark. Whiskers probably originated with pantotheres, because egg-laying mammals don't have them and other mammals do.

The pantothere from Portugal probably resembled a small opossum. Its body was no doubt layered in fat and covered with a dense coat of fur down to its elbows and knees. But like many mammals, such as opossums and rats, its lower legs and tail may have remained thin and scaly. In this way the pantothere could either tuck in its legs and tail to keep warm or extend them to cool off. Pantotheres kept their upper arms and thighs tucked in close to the body. Sometimes it is hard to find a small mammal's elbows and knees because they are enclosed within the skin of the torso.

The Portuguese pantothere had

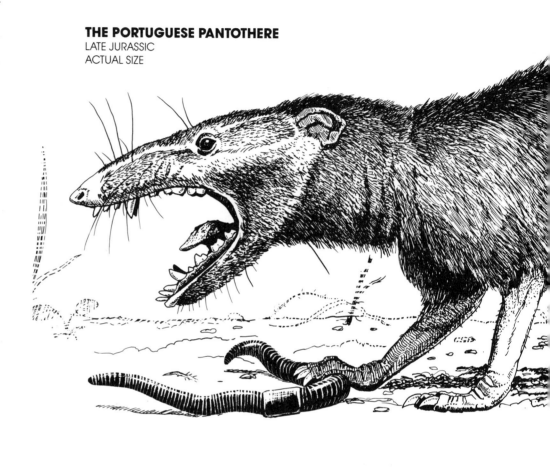

THE PORTUGUESE PANTOTHERE
LATE JURASSIC
ACTUAL SIZE

marsupial bones (see illustration page 80). These are bones that appear in front of the pelvis of early mammals. An inner thigh muscle originates from there in living egg layers. In pouched mammals, marsupial bones serve as belly stiffeners, to prevent a loaded pouch from swinging too much.

Marsupials such as the opossum are examples of how the reproductive process occurred in pantotheres. Opossums produce eggs provided with a shell membrane and a small yolk, but these eggs never grow larger than the head of a pin, and they are never laid. The tiny yolk is quickly

used up. The embryo continues to absorb nutrients from its mother's uterus through a simple placenta.

Two weeks after fertilization, birth occurs. While giving birth, the mother lies on her back. The babies are expelled onto the base of her tail. Blind, naked, and underdeveloped, the fetuses climb without assistance up to their mother's teats, or nipples. A teat is the outlet of a milk gland, shaped to fit a baby's mouth.

Sometimes there are more babies born than there are teats to go around. The babies that reach the teats successfully don't let go for many months

What's New?

Molars with three cusps arranged in
  reversed triangles
Arms tucked in close to ribs
Larger overall size
Marsupial bones
Probable:
  Hearing more acute
  External earflaps
  Whiskers
  Live birth
  Teats (nipples)
  Double vagina
  Anus separate from urine/birth
    canal
  Scrotum

afterward. During this time they quietly grow and develop as they are carried everywhere their mother goes.

Primitive marsupials have many offspring. They breed often, usually right after giving birth. Reproducing this way assures their survival.

In female marsupials the anus is separated from the birth and urine canal. This canal is shorter than a cloaca and splits to form twin vaginas (see top left illustration page 87).

The anus is separate in male marsupials as well. The penis remains nearly absent. The penis remains sheathed within the body unless it is extended for mating. In addition to sperm transport, however, the marsupial penis also expels urine.

In most mammals, sperm are produced only if the testicles are kept cooler than body temperature. That is why they descend outside of the body in a sac called a scrotum. In marsupials this bag of skin hangs below the belly in front of the penis. A scrotum and a pouch are the same structures in male and female marsupial embryos. Hormones turn them into different body parts as they mature.

Pantotheres lived during the Jurassic period from 180 million to 140 million years ago in Europe, North America, and East Africa. At that time all three areas were temperate to equatorial parts of the same supercontinent.

Asioryctes—back to the nest.

Humans are eutherians, or "true beasts," mammals that nurture their embryos by means of a complex placenta. This placenta evolved from the allantois (see page 57) of the amniote egg. It attaches to the wall of the mother's uterus, or womb. The placenta's blood vessels and the womb's blood vessels become very close to one another, allowing the exchange of food, water, oxygen, and wastes. After the birth of the baby the placenta (or allantois), chorion sac, and amniotic sac are all discharged and often are eaten by the mother.

In most cases, eutherian young are born in a well-developed state after a fairly long gestation (pregnancy). However, small eutherians, such as shrews and rodents, are born at an immature stage. They are never quite as embryonic in appearance as a new-born marsupial, however.

Development occurs more rapidly in a uterus than in a pouch. A longer uterine development time increases the brain's capacity, which is especially evident in primates and whales. Eutherians generally have a higher metabolism than marsupials. Their nerve signals may work at a faster rate, and they may need larger amounts of food. Generally speaking, eutherians mature more quickly than marsupials. So over time they breed faster and have more offspring. Eutherians have outnumbered other mammals on every continent they have entered (except Australia) since the disappearance of the dinosaurs.

Eutherian embryos develop in a very special way. After growing to a blastula (see page 22), the cells divide into an inner mass, which will become the baby, and an outer layer, which will become the placenta (see middle illustration page 87). The placenta

ASIORYCTES
LATE CRETACEOUS
ACTUAL SIZE

grows into the lining of the uterus. It also sends a hormone to the mother's body that prepares it for pregnancy. The placenta protects the baby from the mother's immune system. The immune system attacks germs and other foreign organisms that invade the body.

Eutherians probably appeared early in the Cretaceous period. The earliest eutherian fossils so far discovered have come from late Cretaceous rocks.

Asioryctes (ay-zhee-oh-RIK-tees), or "Asian digger," is a model ancestor for all eutherians, from whales and giraffes to humans. The living mammal it most closely resembles is the tree shrew (see page 88).

Asi's shoulder blades, like those of the unnamed Portuguese pantothere, rode loosely over its back. In this way they increased the stride or range of the forelimbs. Asi's upper arm fit into the shoulder socket by way of a ball-and-socket joint, which made it strong and flexible.

What's New?

Mammalian-style shoulder blade
Ball-and-socket shoulder joint
Longer rear limbs
Large springy curve to the back
Marsupial bones absent
Probable:
   Placenta
   Penis bone
   Single vagina
   Palate ridges

THE EVOLUTION OF THE SHOULDER GIRDLE

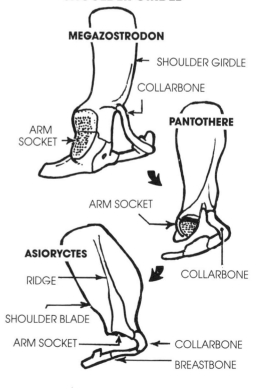

MEGAZOSTRODON
SHOULDER GIRDLE
COLLARBONE
ARM SOCKET

PANTOTHERE
ARM SOCKET
COLLARBONE

ASIORYCTES
RIDGE
SHOULDER BLADE
ARM SOCKET
COLLARBONE
BREASTBONE

A feature that most mammals have is a strong ridge on their shoulder blades. It runs from the arm socket to the opposite edge of the shoulder blade nearest the backbone. You can feel it as you reach over your left shoulder with your right hand. The chest muscle that was used to push up the body when the elbows stuck out to the sides shifted over to the shoulder blade when the forelimbs tucked in close to the body. At the shoulder blade this muscle split in half to line both sides of the ridge, where it continued to support the forelimb in a new way.

Female eutherians have only one vagina, formed by the fusion of the twin vaginas in marsupials. The uteruses remained paired, but their walls thickened to support larger fetuses. Humans have only one uterus, formed from the fusion of the pair.

Most eutherians have a bone inside the penis, which lends support during mating. No eutherians have marsupial bones. Because larger fetuses stretched the belly of pregnant eutherian females, belly-stiffening marsupial bones were phased out.

Hard ridges are to be found on the palate of eutherians. These help in the manipulation of food. You can feel them with your tongue. In baleen whales, these ridges develop into giant fringed plates of "whalebone" for filtering plankton from seawater.

Like a shrew, Asi ate worms and insects and came out only after dark. During a life span of one or two years, Asi might have parented 4 litters of 4 to 7 young. Each pregnancy would have lasted only 4 weeks at a time.

Asi lived during the late Cretaceous period, 84 million years ago, in Mongolia, at that time a temperate part of a northern supercontinent.

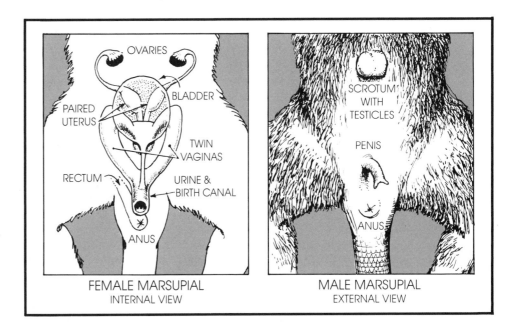

FEMALE MARSUPIAL
INTERNAL VIEW

MALE MARSUPIAL
EXTERNAL VIEW

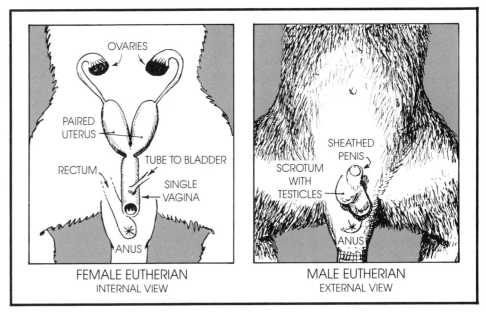

FEMALE EUTHERIAN
INTERNAL VIEW

MALE EUTHERIAN
EXTERNAL VIEW

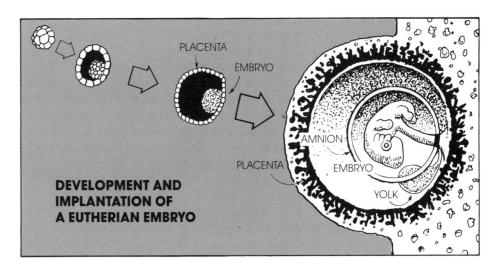

DEVELOPMENT AND
IMPLANTATION OF
A EUTHERIAN EMBRYO

The Tree Shrew—able to grasp food with its bare hands.

The tree shrew looks and acts like a squirrel. Instead of eating nuts and seeds, as squirrels do, it eats insects, as other primitive mammals do. It lives today in Southeast Asian rain forests, and its only known fossils are less than 5 million years old. Nevertheless, tree shrews probably originated before dinosaurs became extinct. Tree shrew skeletons most closely resemble those of mammals like *Asioryctes* (see page 86) of the late Cretaceous period. Blood tests show that they are related most closely to living insectivores (shrews, moles and their kin) and primates (humans, monkeys and their kin). They probably form a link between the two.

Unlike a squirrel, a tree shrew is a hunter that must stalk its prey, pounce on it, and shove it into its mouth for a kill. It must do all this while balancing on a slender branch, where one false move means a fall to the ground. Many primates are insect-eating tree-dwellers that have taken these skills to perfection.

Despite the name "tree shrew," only one type lives in standing trees all the time. The others climb on fallen trees, in low bushes, and on the ground. All tree shrews have the ability to climb and leap.

To move quickly, tree shrews gallop. Galloping is a new way to move, in which all four limbs are in the air at the same time during part of each stride. Basically it involves a series of leaps.

To find food in the dense underbrush, tree shrews rely on their eyes as much as their noses, and on their hands as much as their teeth. This is where a talent for hand-eye coordination improved. Like a primate, a tree shrew has large eyeballs. Each one is protected and supported on the side by a

**COMMON TREE SHREW &
PEN-TAILED TREE SHREW**
PRESENT DAY
ACTUAL SIZE
FOR A SKELETAL VIEW, SEE PAGE 118.

rim of bone. A tree shrew cannot retract its eyeballs into their sockets. Nor does it have a clear third eyelid. Both eyes are angled forward somewhat, giving tree shrews good depth perception. Tree shrews have better color vision than most mammals do, other than primates. It helps them spot hidden insects better. They also have a larger brain to process this visual information.

The pen-tail is the most advanced tree shrew in certain ways. It lives full-time in trees. It has somewhat divergent first digits that give it the ability to grasp objects. Pen-tails use this ability to capture flying insects and to hold them while eating. Some tree shrews' diet includes rodents and lizards, which they kill with a swift and accurate bite to the neck.

Like an opossum, pen-tails have a scaly tail, but the last inch of its tip is

What's New?

Home in bushes and trees
Ability to climb and leap
Eye-hand coordination replacing
  nose-mouth-type feeding
Galloping
Large eyeball
Rim of bone around eyeball
Third eyelid absent
Eye-retractor muscle absent
Eyes angled forward
Color vision
Larger brain
First digits able to grasp
Tails as balancing organs
Tails covered with thick fur
Daylight living with higher tempera-
  ture and metabolism
Longer pregnancy
Fewer breasts (down to one pair)
Penis and testicles side by side
Small range of vocal sounds
Cartilage supports ears
Wet nose, with split upper lip
Feathery extra tongues

decorated with long feathery hairs. Other tree shrews have tails covered

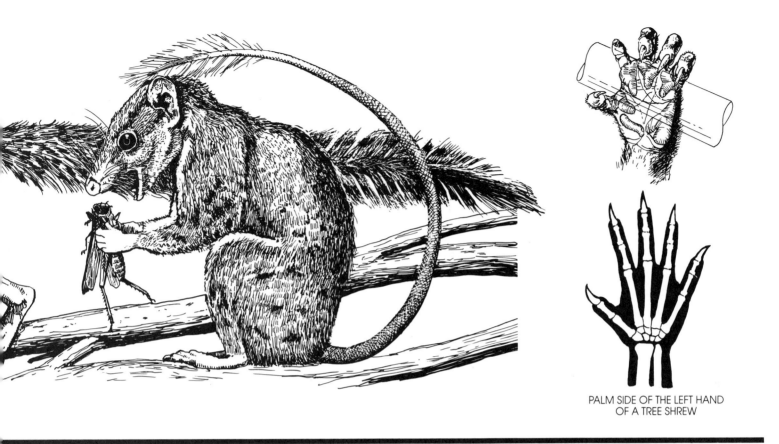

PALM SIDE OF THE LEFT HAND
OF A TREE SHREW

with rich soft fur. A tree shrew uses its tail for balance.

Most tree shrews are active during the daylight. Because they are likely to find high afternoon temperatures, their body temperatures are set at 98.6 degrees Fahrenheit. This is the temperature of humans and most other daylight-living mammals.

Tree shrews have a typically high mammalian metabolism. Like squirrels, they act and react rapidly, pausing only for brief moments in their nervous daily routines. To fuel their energy and heating requirements, tree shrews must eat their own weight in food each day.

Tree shrews hunt alone. They are aggressive to their own kind, except when breeding and nesting. They patrol areas and mark them with scent glands and body wastes. Some scientists think that this mammalian practice can be traced back to early cynodonts.

Tree shrews produce only a few sounds, ranging from a snarling hiss to a piercing squeal. When they are alarmed, they chatter. Most have cartilage that shapes and supports their ears, as in humans.

Males and females are almost identical in size and appearance. Females give birth to between 1 and 3 young after a pregnancy of 50 days. Babies are born naked and with ears and eyes closed. Tree shrew species that give birth to 3 offspring at a time have 3 pairs of breasts. Those that give birth to a single baby have only 1 pair of breasts.

Baby tree shrews are kept in a nest separate from their mothers. They are visited every other day for no more than 10 minutes at a time. After 6 weeks and less than 2 hours of maternal care, the young are weaned. They mature by 4 months.

The male's penis lies side by side with the testicles as a part of the scrotum. Evidently, this was a midpoint in the movement of the scrotum to the rear. In insectivores and marsupials, the scrotum appears on the belly, but in most primates, including humans, it appears behind the penis.

Like a dog, tree shrews have a wet, naked nose. Beneath it, the upper lip is split and tightly attached to the upper jaw. The rest of the muscular lip can be drawn back to expose the teeth underneath, a tree shrew's only facial expression.

An unusal feature of tree shrews, also seen in lemurs (see page 92), is a pair of feathery extra tongues. They are found below the main tongue and are thought to be used as toothbrushes for cleaning the front teeth.

The Primates—take a swing through their family tree.

The chart to the right is an overview of the family tree of primates from 70 million years ago to the present.

What made early primates so special? The answer is, not much. None had hooves or horns. None had flukes or wings. In fact, early primates were about as primitive as the earliest mammals.

Living in the complex world of tree limbs as they did, primates developed a good grasp and good hand-eye coordination. Primates also had the ability to sit on their rumps with their hands free. A dog sniffs and examines objects on the ground, but a primate lifts objects with its hands up to its nose and eyes.

Except for their molars, the earliest known near-primates had no other strictly primate features. They began to appear shortly before the dinosaurs' final extinction. Some of these very common mammals looked like tree shrews (see page 88). Others looked like long-limbed squirrels. After 20 million years all became extinct. Perhaps they lost their low brush habitats to better-adapted rodents.

True primates begin with the Prosimians ("before the apes"). Many, such as lemurs and lorises, are living today.

Adapids were primitive versions of living lemurs. They were at home among the canopy branches of the highest trees. Their long limbs and four grasping "hands" were a big breakthrough. All later primates used their long limbs and "hands" to great advantage. Adapids spread across North America, Europe, and East Asia during the Eocene epoch, before gradually dying out.

Lemurs, which today live only on Madagascar and surrounding African islands, are the bigger-brained, comb-toothed descendants of adapids. Lorises, which are found across southern Asia and Africa, are in turn, the pug-nosed descendants of lemurs.

Tarsiers are small, nocturnal insect predators with owl-like eyes. They are especially good leapers. During the Eocene epoch, tarsier cousins lived in the jungles of Europe and North America. Today tarsiers live only in Southeast Asia.

Monkeys, apes, and tarsiers are called haplorrhines ("single nose") because they all share the characteristic of an uncleft upper lip and a warm, dry nose.

At the end of the Eocene epoch, a sharp drop in worldwide temperatures caused most primates outside the tropics to die out.

At the same time, the bigger brained monkeys and apes, together known as anthropoids ("human-shaped ones"), appeared in many warm equatorial regions around the world.

South and Central America became home for the New World monkeys. Their widely spaced nostrils open to the sides, rather than down. Some have a long prehensile, or grasping, tail, which they employ as a "fifth hand" to swing between branches.

Africa, Europe, and Asia are where Old World monkeys began and live today. They have narrowly spaced nostrils that open downward. Many have cheek pouches and sitting pads, thickened skin on their rear ends.

Stiff-backed hominoids ("resembling humans") include living apes, humans, and their ancestors. Like some lemurs and monkeys, hominoids have lost their tails.

Gibbons perfected a new way to get around, called brachiating. They use their extra-long arms and hooklike hands to swing beneath even the slenderest of branches.

At the end of the Miocene epoch, temperatures warmed and jungle forests once again spread across the globe. Forest apes moved back into Europe, East Asia, and East Africa. Some grew larger than gorillas.

Cool, dry weather patterns returned during the middle of the Miocene epoch. Jungle forests retreated for the last time back to the tropics. Pongids ("ape-types") remained in the shrinking jungles. Among the living pongids are orangutans, which live in Southeast Asian rain forests, and chimps and gorillas, which live in African jungles.

Hominids ("human types") adapted to life in the newly exposed grasslands between the trees. Australopithecines ("southern apes") are the oldest known hominids. They stood erect and had feet they used mostly for walking. In adapting to eating only plants, some australopithecines came to resemble large gorillas.

Hominines (humans and prehumans) are notable for their enlarged brains and their ability to solve almost any problem affecting their lives.

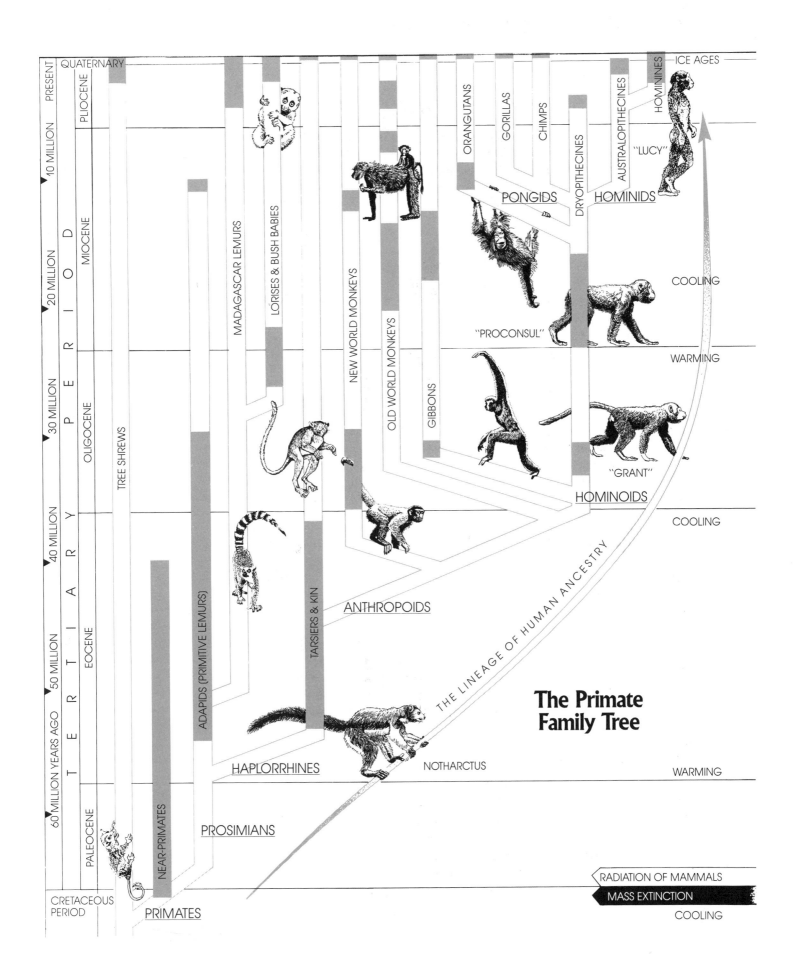

The Primate Family Tree

THE LINEAGE OF HUMAN ANCESTRY

PRIMATES
NEAR-PRIMATES
PROSIMIANS
HAPLORRHINES
ANTHROPOIDS
HOMINOIDS
HOMINIDS
PONGIDS

TREE SHREWS
ADAPIDS (PRIMITIVE LEMURS)
TARSIERS & KIN
MADAGASCAR LEMURS
LORISES & BUSH BABIES
NEW WORLD MONKEYS
OLD WORLD MONKEYS
GIBBONS
ORANGUTANS
GORILLAS
CHIMPS
DRYOPITHECINES
AUSTRALOPITHECINES
HOMININES

NOTHARCTUS
"GRANT"
"PROCONSUL"
"LUCY"

CRETACEOUS PERIOD
PALEOCENE
EOCENE
OLIGOCENE
MIOCENE
PLIOCENE
QUATERNARY

TERTIARY PERIOD

60 MILLION YEARS AGO
50 MILLION
40 MILLION
30 MILLION
20 MILLION
10 MILLION
PRESENT

MASS EXTINCTION
RADIATION OF MAMMALS
COOLING
WARMING
COOLING
WARMING
COOLING
ICE AGES

Adapids—the long-legged daddies of the primates.

The earliest known true primates are primitive lemurs called adapids. In the far-from-complete fossil record, they first appear early in the Eocene epoch, 50 million years ago.

While most primates are known only from their dental remains, long-legged *Notharctus* (noth-ARK-tus), or "false bear," left a nearly complete skeleton.

Like a modern lemur, Notha was a tree dweller. This primate moved rapidly along the tops of large branches, holding on with all four long-fingered "hands." Long fingers wrapped around a branch can support more weight in more positions than short, clawed fingers can. Unlike a squirrel or a tree shrew, a lemur needs only one hand to grasp prey or a branch. Infants gained a firm grip on their mother as they rode around the jungle together. The baby also received a better education than it could sitting in a nest waiting for its mother's return.

About the size of a cat, Notha had long arms and even longer legs. With these it was able to spring from branch to branch across great gaps.

Notha's first toe was well spread apart from the other toes. It wrapped around branches in the opposite direction for a better grasp. While Notha was leaping, its feet acted as landing gear. The first digit on each hand was not yet as thumblike as each first toe.

More primitive than a living lemur, Notha still had claws, not nails. Living lemurs have nails on every digit but 2. A claw remains on each second toe, and it is used for grooming.

Like living lemurs, Notha must have had thin, highly sensitive finger pads rather than the thick ones so typical of ground-dwelling mammals.

Adapids gradually adopted a new

NOTHARCTUS
EOCENE EPOCH
FOR A SKELETAL VIEW
SEE PAGE 118.

way to get from place to place. It is known as vertical clinging and leaping. Many living lemurs rest by clinging upright to slender tree trunks. They find it comfortable to sit erect because their neck bones are at an angle below their skull. From this vertical position they can also leap great distances to other tree trunks. They

What's New?

Larger overall size
Longer arms and legs
Longer digits
Fully opposable big toe
Larger eyes
Shorter snout
Larger brain
Ear bones encased in bone
Probable:
    Vertical clinging and leaping
    Social groups
    Singing and hooting
    Longer pregnancy, childhood,
      and life span
    Vegetation added to diet

NOTHARCTUS
AND
SMILODECTES
ACTUAL SIZE

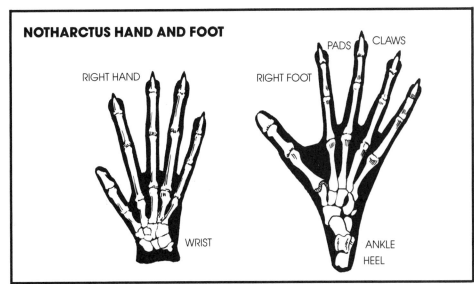

NOTHARCTUS HAND AND FOOT

RIGHT HAND

RIGHT FOOT

PADS   CLAWS

WRIST

ANKLE
HEEL

land feet first with their long bushy tails sailing out behind for balance.

Although plant food was the greatest part of its diet, Notha shoved into its mouth whatever looked good while scrambling through the brush. A modern lemur has a diet that includes shoots, fruit, insects, tree lizards, and eggs.

Notha had a smaller brain than living lemurs but a larger one than that of the near-primates and tree shrews.

Notha's left and right jawbones fused at the "chin," making one solid jawbone, as in humans.

A bony cover encased Notha's tiny middle ear bones in their own little cavern.

Notha had both eyes pointing straight ahead, not out to the sides. Overlapping vision gives depth perception without having to cock the head from side to side to fix the distance in the mind. This is important for stalking prey, as much as for leaping between branches. Insects and lizards are great motion detectors, but seem not to recognize as dangerous a pair of big eyes inching toward them. Squirrels nervously cock their heads from side to side to accurately judge leaping distances. In contrast, lemurs have a steady gaze, like that of a cat.

Notha's sight became more important, but a lemur's habit of marking territories with scent-gland rubbings indicates a continuing importance of the sense of smell. *Smilodectes* was a close relative of Notha's with a smaller snout. The trend toward larger eyes

and a smaller snout shows up in a wide variety of adapid descendents.

Some living lemurs are tiny nocturnal insect eaters. Others are large, are active in daylight, and eat fruit and leaves. Some are nearly tailless. Others have long bushy tails. Some never come to the ground, whereas others are often found there. Some lemurs live alone, but others form social groups of up to 25. Some are silent, whereas others like to sing and hoot. Such sounds may act as threats or as claims to territory. On chilly mornings many lemurs can be found with arms outstretched, warming themselves by basking in the sunlight. As in most primates, the chest, belly, and the insides of the arms and legs are much less hairy than the sides and back.

Lemurs usually have only one baby at a time after a 126-day (18-week) pregnancy. The baby clings to its mother constantly and matures in 18 months. A typical lemur's life span is 18 years.

Notha lived during the Eocene epoch, 50 to 47 million years ago in what is now the western United States. At that time that area was a dense tropical forest.

Grant the Aegyptopithecine—an adapid, monkey, and ape

The ancestor of humans, apes, and perhaps all Old World monkeys as well was a very primitive ape with a tail known as *Aegyptopithecus* (ee-jip-toe-PITH-uh-kuss), the "Egyptian Ape." The first skull of *Aegyptopithecus* ever found was nicknamed Grant, after its discoverer, Grant Meyer. Three later specimens were named Tom, Dick, and Harry. Since these creatures are becoming increasingly human, it seems only reasonable to begin calling them by their nicknames.

Grant resembled a living monkey, but he had the long snout of an adapid (see page 92). No complete skeletons of this early ape have been found. All four skulls so far discovered probably belonged to males. They each had large canines and large molars. Female skulls were probably smaller in size and more fragile. They may have already crumbled to dust.

In living primates, oversized males with large fangs are signs that the animal lives in a troop where the dominance of a leader is important. Such a leader maintains a harem of several females and is the first to battle intruders. The other members of the troop recognize their leader and each other not by smell but by sight. Each troop member has a unique face and body shape. In life, the four aegyptopithecine skulls must have had individually unique faces. One had a shorter snout. Another had a higher skull crest. A third had wider cheekbones.

Like all Old World monkeys and apes, Grant's nostrils opened close together and faced down, not out to the sides as in New World monkeys. Old World monkeys and apes lack catlike whiskers. Their upper lip is uncleft, and it is not bound to the gums beneath. Supplied with facial

muscles, the upper lip moves and contributes to facial expressions.

Grant had 32 teeth, the same number as in humans. The incisors were chisel-shaped, the canines were large and pointed, and the lower molars had a 5-cusp pattern. This last characteristic defines ape and human molars. Grant's canines were so large that they rubbed against one another, honing their edges the way a knife sharpener does.

Grant, like humans, had a full plate of bone completely separating his eyeballs from the bulging jaw muscles in

What's New?

Down to 32 teeth
Incisors chisel-shaped
Molars with 5 cusps
Eyes face completely forward
Bony plate behind eyeballs
Individuals with unique faces
Nails instead of claws
Probable:
  Wider range of facial expressions
  Uncleft upper lip
  Narrowly spaced nostrils
  Whiskers absent
  Hair thinner, less bushy
  Naked face and buttocks
  Detailed vision with special retina
  Buttock pads
  Adaptable, teachable

his temples. If those muscles had pressed against the backs of his eyes,

mix.

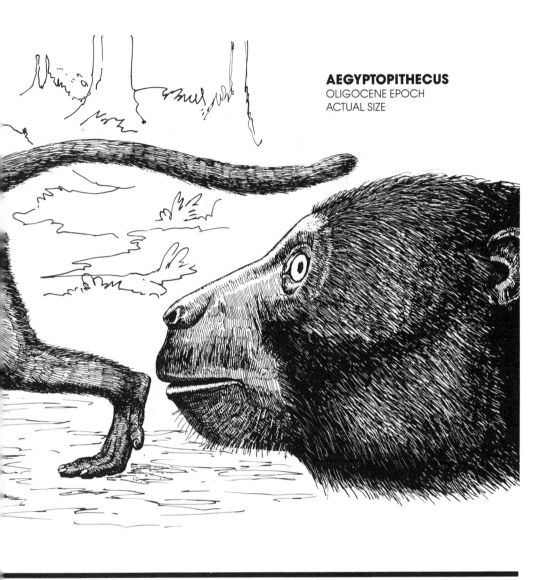

AEGYPTOPITHECUS
OLIGOCENE EPOCH
ACTUAL SIZE

had large, naked, calloused pads. Old World monkeys use them to sit on. Apes, which make nests, have them only occasionally. During the mating season, those on the female often become swollen and brilliantly colored.

Grant was the size of a living lemur and had a tail of unknown length. The small amount of his skeleton that has been found shows an animal more primitive than any living monkey or ape. In other words, except for his face, teeth, and eye sockets, Grant was more adapid than anthropoid.

Grant had a small brain, a little over 1½ cubic inches in volume. It was smaller than that of any living monkey, but larger than that of a lemur.

Considering the angle at which his neck and skull connected, Grant was probably on all fours full-time. Estimated at 11 pounds in weight, Grant was primarily a fruit eater that occasionally ate meat for protein. If that was the case, then this ape was probably a tree climber rather than a ground rover. His thumb would have been well separated from his other fingers for a good grip. His claws would have disappeared, leaving only fingernails and toenails. Nails are the remains of claws, with the bony core removed.

Like most apes and monkeys, Grant was most likely awake at dawn and asleep after sunset. Apes tend to be not so sensitive to changing temperature as lemurs are. They are also able to learn from their companions and to share newfound knowledge.

Grant lived during the early Oligocene epoch, 33 million years ago, in Egypt. What is now a barren desert was then a lush, tropical, vine-covered forest, bordering rivers, streams, and lakes.

they would have thrown his vision out of focus.

Apes and monkeys have excellent color vision because they have many color-sensing cells in their retinas. The retina is the light-sensitive layer inside each eye. A special part of each retina focuses details for extra-sharp vision. This is the area that helps us read fine details.

Apes have thinner hair than lemurs, and what they do have is less bushy. Naked skin shows up on the buttocks and the face. This last feature helped others read Grant's facial expressions.

Sometimes the skin of monkeys can be quite colorful. Mandrills, with their red, white, and blue faces, are perhaps the most striking. Genitals can also be bright red or blue. Reds are produced by the color of blood near the surface. Blues are produced by clear skin cells that refract only blue light.

Strong emotions bring skin colors to their peak intensity. Humans blush, redden with anger, and become paler with fear, revealing their emotions through color.

On the buttocks, Grant probably

Proconsul the dryopithecine—the great granddaddy of the

Proconsul's skull looked so much like that of a chimpanzee to his discoverers that he was named after Consul, a London Zoo chimp of the 1940s.

According to blood tests, 98 percent of a human's DNA is identical to that of a chimp. Before the human and chimp lineages went their separate ways, Proconsul may have been the last ancestor they both shared in common.

Proconsul's scientific name is *Dryopithecus* (dry-oh-PITH-uh-kuss), or "oak ape." During the early Miocene epoch, oak apes came in many sizes. They outnumbered monkeys 20 to 1, just the opposite of the present situation.

Like *Aegyptopithecus* (see page 94), Proconsul had ape teeth but otherwise was similar to an Old World monkey.

Proconsul's canines were large. Apes use their large canines as weapons for self-protection. They also use them to discourage rivals. They do not use them for killing prey. Apes use their fangs for piercing the outer skins of tough fruits and to strip vegetation.

The skull of Proconsul was round and smooth, like a monkey's. No adapidlike muzzle nor apelike brow ridges stuck out from it.

Proconsul had monkeylike limb bones that were probably best suited for running on all fours along tree branches. His hands were similar to a human's. They had not yet evolved into long-fingered, short-thumbed hooks, like those of living apes. So rather than walking on his knuckles, Proconsul walked with all four of his "palms" flat on the ground.

Most mammals keep their elbows tucked in against their ribs. Proconsul's arm joints were loose enough to permit him to hang by his hands alone, with his arms over his head.

Proconsul did this to hoist himself to higher branches in the trees. Experts disagree, however, whether or not this ape was able to brachiate. Brachiating is an ape's way of moving among tree branches by swinging hand over hand. The body dangles below by the shoulders. Children brachiate on "monkey bars" and "jungle gyms." The advan-

What's New?

Larger overall size
More flexible shoulder, arm, and
  wrist joints
Tail absent
Rounder skull
Larger brain
Shorter snout
Probable:
  Fewer backbones
  Part-time ground dweller
  Part-time brachiator
  Appendix
  Buttock pads absent

great apes and humans.

DRYOPITHECUS
MIOCENE EPOCH
ACTUAL SIZE
FOR A SKELETAL VIEW, SEE PAGE 119.

narrow chest. The brachiator has a wide, shallow one. So do humans. With this kind of chest, a smaller spinal ridge forms along the middle of the back. It is more comfortable for brachiators to sit against tree trunks and in chairs.

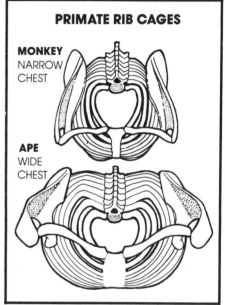

PRIMATE RIB CAGES

MONKEY
NARROW
CHEST

APE
WIDE
CHEST

The tails of Old World monkeys dangle uselessly, for the most part. Tails are absent from many monkeys and all living apes. Proconsul's tail appears to be absent (at least from the fragmented fossil record).

The number of vertebrae in Proconsul's lower back is probably 5 or 6. Living apes have 3 or 4 lower backbones. Humans have 5. Monkeys and lemurs have 7. More bones imply a springy lower back, while fewer bones imply a sturdier one.

Apes don't often have buttock calluses, probably because they build cushiony nests to act as sitting platforms. But buttock and genital swelling may still take place in females during the mating season.

Proconsul lived during the Miocene epoch, 18 million to 14 million years ago, in East Africa. At that time the area was a lush jungle.

tage to this is that brachiators can hang below branches that are far too thin to walk upon. In this way even large brachiators can reach fruit hanging at the very edges of slender branches (where it is most likely to be found).

In many four-footed running mammals, the collarbone disappears

to allow the shoulder blade to move even more freely. In primates it serves as a strut connecting the shoulder blade to the breastbone. Brachiators need their collarbones to anchor important shoulder muscles and to keep their shoulder joints far apart.

The monkey, like most large mammals that run on all fours, has a deep,

The Nut-cracking Prehominid—it took the first steps toward

There is a gap in the fossil record of human ancestry. It occurred between 10 million and 4 million years ago. To fill this gap an imagined primate has been put together based on the features of its known ancestor, *Dryopithecus* (see page 96), its known descendent, *Australopithecus* (see page 102), and its cousins, including chimps.

Human evolution is more than just the evolution of body parts. Learned behavior also evolves. The level of learned behavior in our imagined prehistoric ancestor would have been most similar to that of a chimpanzee living today in its own society and natural habitat. Perhaps chimps give us a glimpse into our own past abilities and behaviors.

Chimpanzees are primarily vegetarians. The enamel on their teeth is thin, so it is suited only for soft plant foods such as fruit and occasionally meat. Chimps hunt and eat bush pigs and other primates when they can. They also savor termites.

Chimps strip twigs and grass to use in fishing termites out of their mounds. Chimps also mash leaves to help sponge up water. To counterattack predators, such as big cats, chimps pick up sticks and stones as weapons. In these ways chimps both use and make tools.

Chimps constantly form and disband social groups. "Friends" greet each other with hugs, kisses, and pats. Chimp society is usually friendly and cooperative. Sometimes, however, packs of chimps wage war against other chimps.

Males may hunt together for small animals and bird eggs. Although at camp males may share their food with females, couples do not pair off permanently.

Chimp pregnancies usually last for 34 weeks, which is twice as long as a lemur's and only 4 weeks short of a human's. Females are sexually mature at 10 years of age. A mother chimp will not mate again as long as her infant is nursing. Infants may nurse to age 5. If infants arrive every 5½ years, a pair of chimps will have only 5 offspring in a typical life span of 40 years.

Not only is the birth rate low, but 40 percent of all chimp babies die while they are still infants. They die for two reasons: lack of interest on the mother's part and injuries from falls. Firstborns suffer more often because of their mother's lack of expe-

rience. In addition to foraging for herself every day, a mother chimp has to carry and care for her young. This burden is not shared by the males. Using all four limbs to get around in the trees and on the ground, a chimp mother cannot hold her baby while foraging. The baby must hold on to its mother for dear life during the long journeys the two make every day.

Our imagined ancestor had a chimp's basic anatomy and life-style. Then it evolved beyond that foundation. Unknowingly it was becoming a hominid, a primate that would someday walk erect like a human.

The first adaptation made by this prehominid broadened its menu. Unlike chimps, a prehominid would have had a short snout, small canines, and molars topped with thick enamel. A tooth pattern like this would have helped them eat hard foods, such as nuts and tough pods. Prehominids could remove the hard rind to get at the rich food inside. Roots (dug with sticks), fruits, eggs, small animals, and scavenged pieces of large carcasses

What's New?

Probable:
  Molars with thick enamel
  Smaller canines
  Semi-erect walking, carrying
  Complex social interactions including kissing, hugging, food sharing, and war
  Tool using, tool making
  Termites and meat in diet
  Longer pregnancy, infancy, maturity, and life span
  Small, flat, naked ears
  "Whites of the eyes" white

becoming a human.

A HYPOTHETICAL PREHOMINID
PLIOCENE EPOCH
PROBABLE ACTUAL SIZE

A CHIMPANZEE
CARRYING
BANANAS

would have rounded out their diet.

With large interlocking fangs, chimps can only grind their molars forward and back. With small canines, prehominids would have been able to grind their teeth from side to side as well, the way humans do.

A prehominid would have looked more like *Dryopithecus* than a chimp. Although it probably was good at climbing trees and hanging by its long hairy arms, it would have spent most of its time foraging on the ground. A prehominid would not have been a limb swinger or a knuckle walker, as chimps are.

In the middle of the Miocene epoch, climates cooled. The rain forests gradually shrank back to the tropics. Grasslands and deserts took their places.

There wasn't enough living space in the jungles, so some apes were forced out. The pongids, or great apes, stayed behind in the shrinking woodlands, while our ancestors, the hominids, made a new home on the opening parklands and grassy areas between the trees. An expanded diet and primitive tools and weapons (digging sticks and clubs) were all the adaptations prehominids needed to succeed in this new environment.

There was a smaller supply of food on the plains than in the same area of forest. A tribe of prehominids had to learn a new way to find food. Males began to search for it farther away from home. In this way they stopped competing with the females and infants for food near the base camp. Because of this, females were able to find all they needed in a smaller area and in fewer hours than before. Fewer miles traveled meant fewer chances of babies falling. Mothers had more time to care for their babies. The death rate

of prehominid babies went down.

Sometimes males would bring back extra food to the base camp and share it with a favorite female. Perhaps in this way sharing partners became lifelong mates. Males who gave food to their mates and offspring helped them survive. Similarly, wolf and bird males help in caring for their young. In these cases the parents are usually partners for life, too. They carry food back to their nest in their belly. Prehominid males could have carried more in their hands.

Chimps are able to stand upright on their hind legs for only short periods of time. They use this ability to see over tall grass and to carry things with their arms and hands. Chimps are not well designed for walking on just two legs. They tire quickly. On the open plains, walking upright became necessary for survival. Those prehominids best suited to the task survived.

Walking is an efficient way to travel long distances without tiring. It also leaves the hands free for carrying items of importance. As a tribe of nomads, prehominids could have carried everything from babies to war clubs to extra food.

In searching for food, hunting techniques must have evolved. One such technique involves staring silently, like a bird dog, at potential prey. It is a natural habit of humans to look where others are looking. This is easily done because the whites of our eyes signal to others exactly where our attention is riveted. Most chimps, like most mammals, have dark-stained "whites." Such eyes are more difficult to follow. When a rare mutation appears that bleaches a chimp's "whites" white, they give the uncanny appearance of being almost human.

The Hominid Family Tree—humans are the only ones left.

The chart to the right is an overview of the hominid family tree from 4 million years ago to the present.

Primates that walk only upon their hind feet are known as hominids ("human types"). Changes in the legs, pelvis, and feet enable hominids to walk erect over long distances. The lower back curves inward to keep the trunk balanced over the hips. The neck is held vertically and joins directly below the skull. Hominids have large molars with high square crowns of thick enamel for eating tough foods. Their canines are not much larger than their incisors.

Hominids split apart from the African pongids (gorillas and chimps) sometime between 15 million and 5 million years ago.

According to fossil footprints and bones, the first ancestor of all known hominids was probably *Australopithecus afarensis*, the "southern ape from the Afar," a region in Ethiopia. In the dry open parklands of East Africa, this hominid with the head and brains of an ape walked fully upright more than 3 million years ago.

Over time, the australopithecine branch became chiefly vegetarian and developed tremendously strong jaw muscles for dealing with tough foods.

The hominine (or "human") branch of hominids ate a meaty diet. Hominine teeth are smaller but stronger, built for tearing meat, tendon, and skin from a carcass. Hominines grew increasingly dependent on tools made from plants, animal skins, animal bones, and stones.

Hominines appear in the fossil record in three waves. Each one had a larger brain and smaller teeth and jaws than the one that came before it (See pages 102-111).

Homo habilis lived side by side with the early australopithecines. It is likely that "capable man" made his own cutting stones by crudely chipping them against one another.

Homo erectus made stone hand axes, wooden spears, and fire. During the 1 million years of his existence, "upright man's" brain grew larger. So did the area of his travels.

Homo sapiens first appeared 300,000 years ago. Not much is known about "wise man" until about 100,000 years ago. At that time a European subspecies appeared. Because he buried his dead (which helped fossilize his bones), we have a better picture of his life than that of his contemporaries.

The African subspecies *Homo sapiens sapiens* ("wise wise man") is first known from cave litter that is 100,000 years old. The oldest known skeleton of "wise wise man" is 35,000 years old. It comes from France, where this human is known as Cro-Magnon (crow-MAN-yon) man. About 35,000 years ago our ancestors took the final great leap forward by evolving the ability to speak in a very complex manner. Ideas were shared more easily, which led to increased cooperation and trade.

In the last 10,000 years, "Wise wise man" has expanded to all the continents and separated into a variety of races. This subspecies is the only one of the hominids that survives to this day.

Humans became farmers. They tamed wild animals. They formed villages and began to record their daily lives as history.

Today human evolution continues. However, no changes have appeared yet that would put anyone into the category of another separate species. Too little time has gone by for such a major change to appear. The evolution of our civilization, on the other hand, has been rapid. There have been new inventions, new fashions, new governments, and new ways of thinking about things appearing every decade.

Walking upright imposed stresses on the legs and abdomen that had never been experienced by any ancestor of the hominids. The stress of moving blood up the legs back to the heart weakens some blood vessels creating varicose veins. The stress of carrying the weight of the abdomen on top of the hips leads to hernias. On the other hand, hominids can dance, which is something few apes have even tried.

There is no direct evidence that any hominid other than *Homo sapiens sapiens* still exists at the present. There are, however, intriguing reports of huge hominids still living in the Pacific Northwest United States and in the Himalayas of Tibet and Nepal in Asia. Footprints, photographs, and eyewitness reports describe these phantom beings as walking upright and standing about seven feet tall or more. They are said to be quite hairy and shy. No bones or other hard evidence of these hominids has ever been found, so their existence has yet to be proven.

Eyewitnesses also report that alien beings arriving on UFOs seem to be hominids, too. These come in a variety of shapes and sizes. Some are said to be very good looking while others are said to have large heads and small bodies. Once again, until hard evidence comes to light, the existence of such creatures remains unproven.

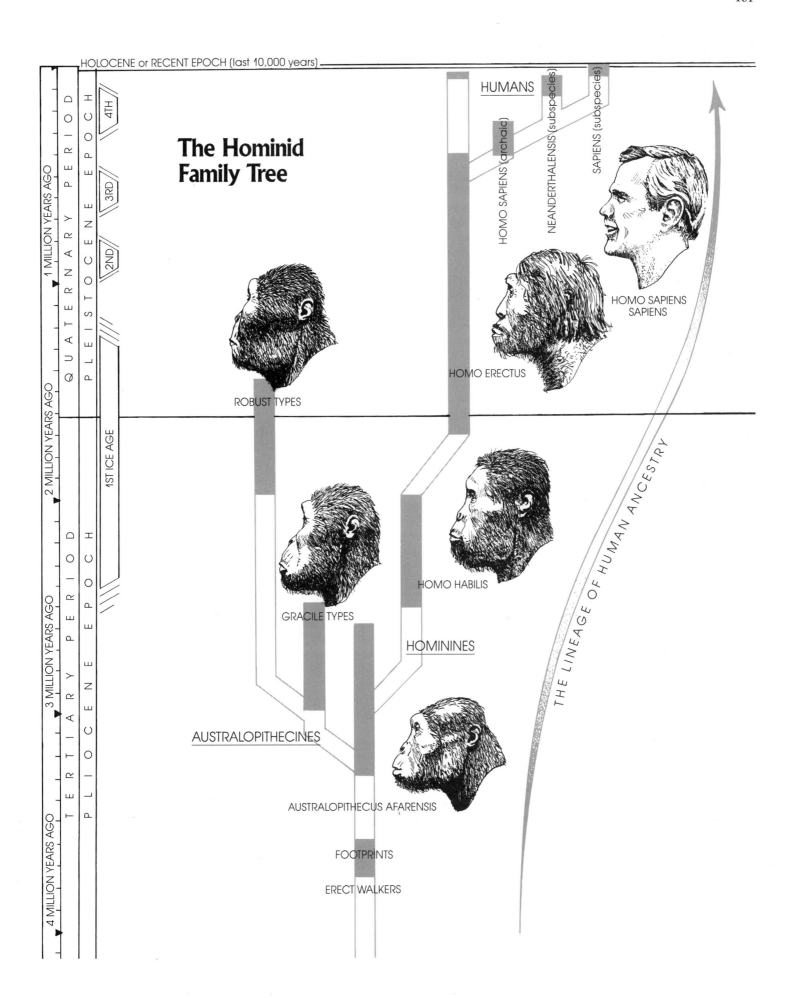

HOLOCENE or RECENT EPOCH (last 10,000 years)

The Hominid Family Tree

HUMANS

HOMO SAPIENS (archaic)

NEANDERTHALENSIS (subspecies)

SAPIENS (subspecies)

HOMO SAPIENS SAPIENS

HOMO ERECTUS

ROBUST TYPES

HOMO HABILIS

GRACILE TYPES

HOMININES

AUSTRALOPITHECINES

THE LINEAGE OF HUMAN ANCESTRY

AUSTRALOPITHECUS AFARENSIS

FOOTPRINTS

ERECT WALKERS

1 MILLION YEARS AGO

2 MILLION YEARS AGO

3 MILLION YEARS AGO

4 MILLION YEARS AGO

QUATERNARY PERIOD

TERTIARY PERIOD

PLEISTOCENE EPOCH

PLIOCENE EPOCH

4TH

3RD

2ND

1ST ICE AGE

Lucy the Australopithecine—she had an ape's head on a

For many years it was assumed that a human's superior brain appeared first on an apelike body. The discovery of *Australopithecus* (aws-truh-lo-PITH-uh-kuss), or "southern ape," fossils proved that just the opposite was true. A semicomplete skeleton was discovered in East Africa. Between 2.6 and 3.3 million years old, it was given the nickname "Lucy" after a popular Beatles song. Other bones and human-looking footprints have been discovered from a close relative walking in volcanic ash 3.6 to 3.8 million years ago.

Lucy inhabited dry, open parklands near wooded lakeshores. She walked almost completely upright, like a human. Unlike the thumblike first toe of an ape, her first toe was like that of a human. It lined up with the other toes. It acted with the other toes to provide push-off power to each of her steps.

Other primate babies grab on to their mother's hair with all four of their "hands." Lucy's babies weren't able to do this with their humanlike feet. They had to be carried. With her arms free, Lucy was able to do this.

Lucy did not hold her head fully erect. Her neck joined farther toward the back of her skull than in humans.

Lucy had large, nut-cracking molars covered with thick enamel. With these she ate a wide variety of difficult-to-chew foods. Her canines were not much different from those of males, and in no case were they fang-like. The lower part of her face was a muzzle. Her cheekbones were broadened by large jaw muscles.

Lucy was knock-kneed, like a human, rather than bowlegged as all chimps are. The shape of her knees kept her center of balance beneath her hips while walking. Lucy's pelvis was more like a human's than an ape's, but

her birth canal wasn't large. The babies of early hominids had small brains that did not require a large birth canal, as big-brained human babies do.

Lucy's brain size of 27 to 36 cubic inches is about one-fourth larger than that of a chimp of the same size. It was about a third as large as a human's.

At 25 years old, Lucy stood about 3 feet 8 inches tall and weighed 65 pounds. Her mate would have been about 5 feet tall and weighed 120 pounds. A smaller body size meant that female hominids needed less to eat than males. Females probably looked for food over a smaller area than males did. The burden of an infant or two would have also cut down on the distance a female traveled. The larger size of the male enabled him to cover more ground with each stride. A larger size also helped against predators.

As male chimps grow up, they form into packs ruled by a pack leader. Such packs are necessary for attack and defense against rival packs. On the other hand, as female chimps mature, they join new tribes. This prevents inbreeding and keeps the tribe male-oriented.

Within a group, there are more chances for learning. Lucy would have learned how to observe and imitate behavior. She probably stayed near the camp with other females, grooming and nursing her own young. Females probably searched the local area for nuts, roots, berries, and other foods. Males probably took off for the frontier, collecting and scavenging whenever possible. By throwing sticks, rocks, and dry uprooted bushes, they might have driven vultures and hyenas away from large carcasses.

The first uniquely hominid tools were probably not hunting weapons,

human body.

▲ FOOTPRINT IN VOLCANIC ASH

AUSTRALOPITHECUS AFARENSIS
◀ FEMALE AND INFANT
PLIOCENE EPOCH
ABOUT ONE-FIFTH ACTUAL SIZE
FOR A SKELETAL VIEW, SEE PAGE 119.

What's New?

Larger brain
Upright posture
Walking on hind legs alone
Nondivergent big toe
Knock-knees
Humanlike pelvis, enlarged buttock
   muscles
Probable:
   Nomadic tribal culture
   Collecting, scavenging
   Higher reproductive rate
   Lower infant mortality rate
   Loss of seasonal mating battles
   Pair bonding
   Loss of penis bone
   Thinning hair
   Increasing ability to sweat
   Human hair patterning
   Better throwing ability

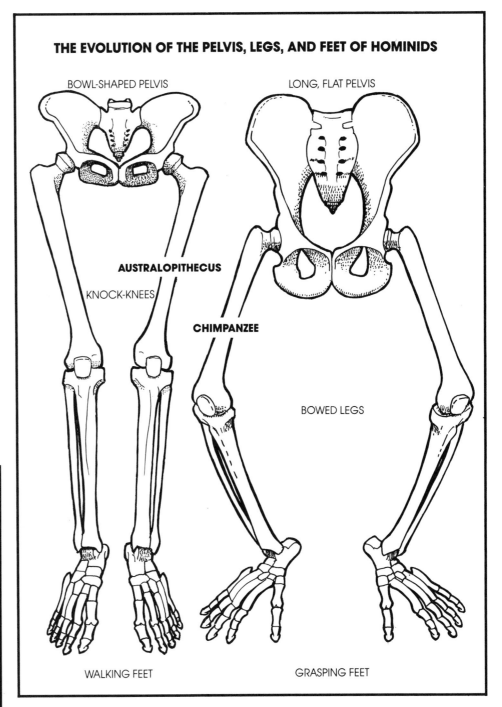

THE EVOLUTION OF THE PELVIS, LEGS, AND FEET OF HOMINIDS

BOWL-SHAPED PELVIS

LONG, FLAT PELVIS

AUSTRALOPITHECUS

KNOCK-KNEES

CHIMPANZEE

BOWED LEGS

WALKING FEET

GRASPING FEET

but sun-dried animal skins used for collecting food.

Lucy's tribe, like those of apes and baboons, was probably nomadic. The tribe probably moved to a new foraging outpost daily and almost never slept in the same spot two nights in a row.

Among chimpanzees and other apes, the bond between mother and young remains strong throughout life. Males are not involved in child rearing. When male hominids took on the role of parent, they became much more successful at reproducing themselves. Parenthood also helped the mating

Lucy the Australopithecine, continued.

partners to form more lasting bonds. In that way, females and infants were assured of food. Males were assured that their mates' offspring were theirs also. When the male helped his mate-for-life, he was helping his own children to survive, too.

The safety of the tribe, combined with food brought in by a mate, meant that speed and tree climbing were no longer of first importance to Lucy's survival. Walking erect was more important. An erect posture made it easier for Lucy to carry a baby in one arm and have one arm free, perhaps for a second infant. When they were able to care for more than one offspring at a time, the hominid's reproductive rate increased. Even twins could survive. Today, the human rate of reproduction is about 5 times that of apes.

A typical female primate experiences changes in her body when her eggs have matured and are ready to be fertilized. Her genitals swell and they send out an odor. Only a female human does not show a change when she becomes fertile. Lucy was probably more like a modern human in this regard.

In most primate societies, every male knows when a female in the area is fertile and receptive to mating. If more than one male shows an interest, fights for dominance usually result. Those that maintain a harem of females guard them fiercely from other males.

That system works fine for apes because they never wander far from their harems in search of food. In the case of hominids, however, a lot of time was spent searching for food, and the males had to go far from camp to look for it. They could not remain home guarding their females against

rivals. In addition, they could not afford to lose the cooperation of their hunting partners by fighting with them over mating partners.

The lifetime bonding of one male with one female has evolved as the best way to keep peace within the tribe. In an ideal situation, each male can count on a faithful mate and each female has a faithful food provider.

It was the fertility signals that drove the males into a frenzy during the short mating season. Lucy had to remain fertile in order to reproduce, but the fertility signals had to stop to reduce the fighting among the males.

Female hominids became more like women. In time they became receptive to mating throughout the year, not just whenever they were fertile. By mating every so often throughout the year, hominids still had a good chance of becoming pregnant by accident. Nature increased the odds by making hominids fertile more often, a few days every month.

In most primate societies, males do not try to attract females. Instead, they try to repel other males from the area by a display of their large canine fangs. Male hominids did not have large fangs to repel rivals. Instead, the human male strategy is to attract the female as a mating partner just as much as the female attracts the male.

It took time for females and males to decide to make their bond permanent (despite love at first sight). Humans usually go through a courtship period in order to get to know one another as individuals and establish trust.

In all human societies the hair on one's head is considered an attractive feature. On other parts of the body, having little or no hair is often considered attractive. Humans have as many

hairs as apes, but over most of the body each one is so tiny that one can say humans are essentially nude. Hair became thinner on later hominids to prevent overheating while hiking long distances under a hot equatorial sun.

What looks like normal primate hair grows on the human scalp, where it forms a sort of sun cap. What makes it unusual is that old hairs do not fall out to be replaced by new ones. They keep growing throughout a lifetime. In both apes and humans the hair grays with old age.

Human males usually grow hair on their face when they reach sexual maturity. Facial hair also never stops growing. In humans of both sexes, hair in the armpits and groin area also appears at maturity. Hair in these regions prevents chafing while walking and mating. These regions are also the sites of the strongest human body odors, and hair traps these odors.

Over most of the human body, the pattern of hair growth is similar to that of apes. In some areas, however, patterns have changed to form runoff channels for excess sweat, such as in front of the ears and at the back of the neck.

Humans can sweat much more than most apes. Sweat cools the skin as it evaporates. This system works best on hairless skin.

Some chimps have black faces, others have pink or brown faces, and a few have a mottled combination of the two. Whatever color hominid skin originally was, it probably darkened by the time Lucy arrived. As hair continued to thin, protective tanning pigments would have increased to resist sunburn.

AUSTRALOPITHECUS
ACTUAL SIZE

Louis and Eugene, Two Early Hominines—a rock hound and

About 2.5 million years ago, Earth entered the first of four Pleistocene Ice Ages. As climates cooled, African forests once again shrank and scrub-brush grasslands took their place. Antelope first appear at this time in the fossil record, along with other species adapted to these drier conditions. Watching them from the shade was the first member of our own genus, *Homo habilis*, or "capable man."

The differences between Louis (nicknamed for his discoverer, Louis Leakey) and *Australopithecus*, (see page 102) were not great. Louis's brain size had increased up to 41 cubic inches. This increase came about by filling out a pinched-in portion of his skull at the temples and raising his forehead a bit. An area of the brain responsible for speech and manual dexterity (finger agility) first appears at this time.

Filling out the temples with brains made Louis's jaw muscles smaller. His molars were narrower, reflecting a change to a more meaty diet. Meat is more nutritious than plant food and Louis could survive by eating less. Near the site of Louis's remains have been found lava cobbles with one end chipped to a point. These crude hand axes are the oldest stone tools one can identify. They were used in many ways, including to break animal bones to get at the marrow. The sharp left-over chips worked well as knives.

From the shape of these tools, we know that Louis was right-handed. He probably slept in trees, using his long arms to hoist himself into the branches. He probably matured quickly, becoming a parent in his teens and old by age 30. Males seem to have been much larger than females. Currently, the fossil record of *Homo habilis* comes to an end 2 million years ago.

HOMO ERECTUS
PLEISTOCENE EPOCH
ONE-SIXTH ACTUAL SIZE

a fireman.

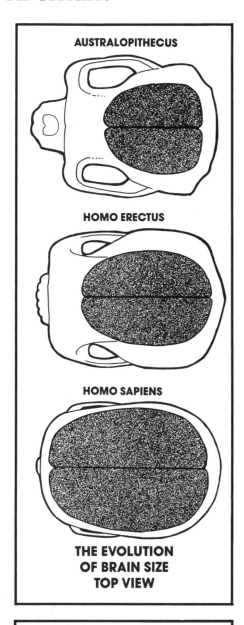

AUSTRALOPITHECUS

HOMO ERECTUS

HOMO SAPIENS

THE EVOLUTION OF BRAIN SIZE TOP VIEW

What's New?

Larger overall size
Larger brain
Crude stone tools
Use of fire
Smaller molars
Longer legs
Shorter arms
Eyebrow ridges
Probable longer life span

Homo erectus, or "upright man," first appeared 1.7 million years ago. At this time there was a warming period between the first two Ice Ages. Eugene (nicknamed for his discoverer, Eugene Dubois) grew to over 6 feet in height, which is taller than most living humans.

Compared with Louis, Eugene had shorter arms and longer legs. In fact, he would have fit into modern clothing. But his face had a wide, apelike nose, a jutting muzzle, and absolutely no chin. To top it off, his thick skull had little or no forehead and an apelike ridge ran across his brow.

Homo erectus spread across Europe, Africa, and Asia, all the way to Indonesia. One had a brain size of 67 cubic inches, more than 60 percent larger than that of his immediate ancestor. Social activity between family and tribal members, both at camp and in the field, probably caused this large increase in brain size. The ability to deceive others and to detect deception probably appeared at this time. In contrast, Eugene's stone-chipping skills show no big advances from his origin to his extinction, which took place over a million years.

Brain size alone is not an absolute indicator of intelligence. Talent and genius have more to do with the quality of brain connections.

There is a limit to how large a brain can get. A large-brained baby can die and kill its mother during birth if her pelvis is not large enough to let it pass through. Until recently, childbirth had been the number-one killer of young women. Women's hipbones may have reached their maximum width without hampering their ability to walk. If this is true, then a baby's brain is limited in size to about 21 cubic inches. In apes, as in most animals, brain size only doubles from birth to adulthood. In humans, it quadruples.

Modern humans are the slowest growing and longest-lived of all the primates. Pregnancy lasts for 38 weeks; nursing may continue up to the age of 5 or 6 in some cultures. Sexual maturity occurs anywhere between the 11th and 16th year. Human females typically cease to produce eggs at around age 50 (although 65-year-old mothers are on record). A human life span usually lasts into the 70s, and a lucky few pass 110.

It takes a long while to learn survival skills. A longer life span has developed because tribes with members who live longer have tended to succeed on the wisdom of their elders.

Eugene learned to use fire: 700,000 years ago he carried glowing embers in hide sacks to make fire wherever he went. Fire helped Eugene bring the heat he knew from the tropics north to the colder climates of Asia and Europe.

Fire also cooks food. Cooking makes meats and vegetables softer and easier to eat. Foods Eugene could not eat raw were now on his menu. Because of his new diet, Eugene's molars had become smaller than those of Louis.

In present-day hunter-gatherer societies, women provide food in the form of roots, berries, grains, and other collected plants. The men bring home rats, turtles, baby animals, and other small prey. They seldom go in search of big game. But that doesn't mean that Eugene would pass up the chance to butcher a fresh elephant trapped in a bog. Perhaps Eugene's tribe drove one there by setting fires to the surrounding reeds. This event was preserved in the fossil record 500,000 years ago.

Early Homo Sapiens—finally learned to eat seafood.

The final chapters in human evolution involve fewer changes in the body and more cultural changes. What humans were doing was becoming more important than the changes in their bodies.

About 500,000 years ago, during the warm period between the second and third Ice Ages, the earliest examples of our own species, *Homo sapiens*, or "wise man," first appeared around the Mediterranean Sea. Anatomically, Mr. Wiseman had a larger braincase, a higher forehead, and smaller teeth than his predecessor, *Homo erectus*. Otherwise there was little difference.

When the third and fourth Ice Ages chilled northern Europe, some humans remained who were adapted to the cold. Others spread south and east to Africa and Asia. By 100,000 years ago, Mr. Wiseman had spread throughout the Old World. Continental boundaries then divided him into three distinct groups.

There are too few human bones from Asia to say much about them. It can be noted that they are different from those of the other two subspecies. Members of different subspecies, such as wolves and dogs, look different but are still able to interbreed.

Our own ancestors, the subspecies *Homo sapiens sapiens*, or "wise wise man," came from southern Africa (see page 110). Caves from that time show seal and penguin bones, along with mollusc shells. This is the first time we know of humans eating seafood. A study of the mammal bones in these caves suggest that these early hunters avoided dangerous prey in face-to-face battle. Instead, large numbers of bones suggest that early humans had killed a whole herd of antelope at once, perhaps by driving them over a cliff.

The cold-adapted human subspecies

HOMO SAPIENS (ARCHAIC)
PLEISTOCENE EPOCH
ABOUT ONE-EIGHTH ACTUAL SIZE

that lived in Europe is the one best known today. From 130,000 to 32,000 years ago, *Homo sapiens neanderthalensis*, or "Neander Valley Wise Man," existed. He lived just south of the glaciers that were chilling Europe during the last two Ice Ages. Mr. Neandertal was strong, thick-boned, and short-legged, like living northern peoples. He had a large face and heavy brows. His brain was larger than ours by 10 percent, but

What's New?

Higher cranium
Smaller brow ridges
Diet includes seafood
Wooden weapons evident
Dead are buried
Sick and aged are cared for

it was set back lower in his skull. Heavy neck muscles were needed to balance his head on top of his spine.

In addition to simple stone tools, Mr. Neandertal made wooden ones,

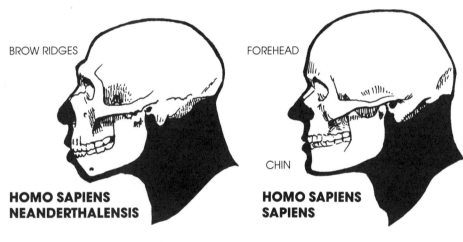

THE BASE OF THE SKULL AND VOICE BOX IN A CHIMP AND A HUMAN

**HOMO SAPIENS
NEANDERTHALENSIS**

**HOMO SAPIENS
SAPIENS**

such as spears. Bundles of animal furs served as clothing to protect these humans from the bitter cold.

During the course of Mr. Neandertal's existence, there was little development of new or refined tools. Mr. Neandertal was not a great wanderer, and he could not speak as well as a modern human can. If he had a new idea, it was not communicated to people in other tribes who could have added to that idea.

Communication skills speed up the spread of new ideas. *Homo habilis* had a brain with a speech center, but his voice box was probably not capable of making a wide range of sounds. In apes and human infants, the voice box is high in the throat. In neither case are they able to produce many of the vowel sounds of adult speech. In both cases a high voice box helps them to keep breathing without a danger of choking while they nurse. As infancy ends in humans, the voice box drops halfway down the neck. At the same time, the skull develops a notch in its

base, which means this feature can be noted in fossils. The earliest time this notch appears is with *Homo sapiens sapiens*, not *Homo sapiens neanderthalensis.*

The remains of Mr. Neandertal are relatively numerous because he helped the fossil process. He buried his dead. Comrades put in his grave many of the possessions the dead person had used during life. Some of the bodies show signs of having suffered through disease for quite some time, indicating that Mr. Neandertal cared for his sick and elderly. However, few lived past age 45.

Modern Homo Sapiens—a new face worth talking about.

The last common ancestor of every living human being probably walked the earth 100,000 years ago in East Africa (see page 108). This mother of humanity, called Eve by Adam in the Bible, was the first member of our own subspecies, called *Homo sapiens sapiens* by scientists worldwide.

Eve had a smaller face and more slender arms and legs than a typical Neandertal. Her face was under her forehead, not in front of it. She had no brow ridges and her muzzle had practically disappeared. Eve had a more slender neck than a Neandertal because her skull was better balanced on top of her spine.

Eve had a chin, a shelf of bone that protruded from the end of her slender lower jaw to strengthen it. Apes also have a strengthening shelf, but it lies on the inside of the jaw.

Eve's nose was erect and protruding, shaped by cartilage. Her nostrils were small, close together, and opened below the tip. With this nose, humans can submerge themselves underwater, something nearly all apes avoid. So long as the air pressure inside the nostrils equals the water pressure, water does not enter the nose and air does not bubble out. The water-loving proboscis monkey also has a protruding nose with nostrils opening beneath it. (For an interesting comparison, see *Panderichthys* pages 48-49.)

Eve had eyebrows, tufts of hair over each eye that no apes have. They act as traps for forehead sweat and as eye shades, but mostly they are used for communication. A raised eyebrow can deliver a message faster than words.

Human lips are not simply mobile tissues that seal off the mouth. They have a different color and texture from the surrounding skin. Lips added an appeal to Eve's face. They also helped

HOMO SAPIENS SAPIENS
PLEISTOCENE EPOCH TO PRESENT DAY
FOR A SKELETAL VIEW, SEE PAGE 119.

her communicate in three ways: by forming sounds, by their role in facial expressions, and by kissing.

About 35,000 years ago, modern humans appeared in France and other places. Their presence is marked by fast changes in civilization. New tools, weapons, and ways of doing things suddenly came into being. There was a skill and artistry never seen before. Humans were learning and communicating at a fast rate. And they were trading with one another over long distances. An ability to speak and communicate may have been the rea-

What's New?

Eyebrows
Larger forehead
Chin
Erect nose
Swimming
Greater travel
Voice box drops
Greater communication skills
Combination wood and stone tools
  and weapons
Dog domesticated
Big game hunted
Rope used
Sewn clothing
Jewelry
Artworks and musical instruments

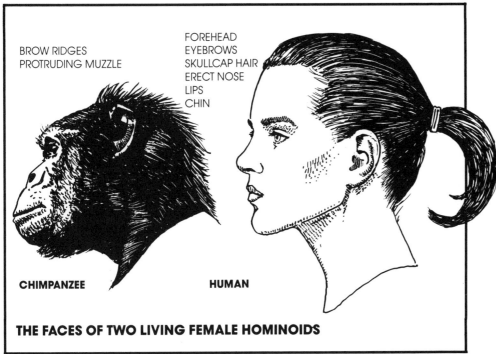

BROW RIDGES
PROTRUDING MUZZLE

FOREHEAD
EYEBROWS
SKULLCAP HAIR
ERECT NOSE
LIPS
CHIN

CHIMPANZEE   HUMAN

THE FACES OF TWO LIVING FEMALE HOMINOIDS

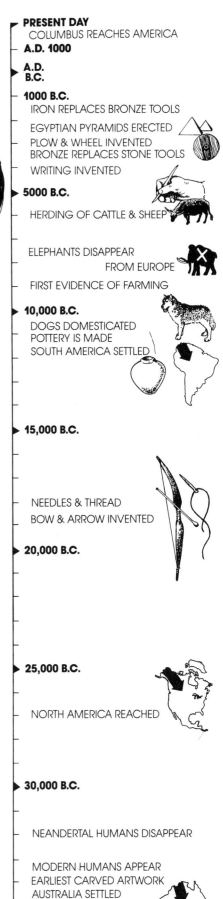

PRESENT DAY
COLUMBUS REACHES AMERICA
A.D. 1000
A.D.
B.C.
1000 B.C.
IRON REPLACES BRONZE TOOLS
EGYPTIAN PYRAMIDS ERECTED
PLOW & WHEEL INVENTED
BRONZE REPLACES STONE TOOLS
WRITING INVENTED
5000 B.C.
HERDING OF CATTLE & SHEEP

ELEPHANTS DISAPPEAR
FROM EUROPE
FIRST EVIDENCE OF FARMING
10,000 B.C.
DOGS DOMESTICATED
POTTERY IS MADE
SOUTH AMERICA SETTLED

15,000 B.C.

NEEDLES & THREAD
BOW & ARROW INVENTED
20,000 B.C.

25,000 B.C.

NORTH AMERICA REACHED

30,000 B.C.

NEANDERTAL HUMANS DISAPPEAR

MODERN HUMANS APPEAR
EARLIEST CARVED ARTWORK
AUSTRALIA SETTLED
35,000 B.C.

son for these rapid changes.

As Eve's skull became highly domed, speech and higher-reasoning centers were the parts of her brain that expanded the most. Her brain size increased to between 73 and 88 cubic inches.

Reindeer, bison, and mammoth all lived within sight of Adam and Eve. Adam liked to hunt reindeer best, but he pursued and ate all the animals. His weapons included the spear thrower, the barbed harpoon, and later, the bow and arrow.

Early people carved tools from bone and antlers. They tied or glued wooden handles on stone tools to increase their leverage. Some must have made nets, because the bones of small swift rabbits, birds, and fish litter certain caves.

About 18,000 years ago people began to sew clothing with needles made of bone and ivory. Furs and skins were the original outerwear. Necklaces of gems, shells, bone, and feathers were the first jewelry.

Adam and Eve had plenty of free time, which they devoted to play, the arts, and religion. They made musical instruments ranging from rattles to flutes. They engraved beautiful designs into bone and ivory. Their cave paintings and clay figurines may have been objects of worship rather than mere works of art.

Shortly after *Homo sapiens sapiens* arrived in Europe, the *Homo sapiens neanderthalensis* subspecies became extinct. Perhaps they were killed through competition or by epidemic diseases. The history of modern humans is filled with equally tragic exterminations.

During the last glacial age, lower sea levels provided land bridges between the continents. By 11,000 years ago tribes had settled into all the continents but one. Antarctica was first sighted in 1820 and explored shortly thereafter. In 1969, *Homo sapiens sapiens* first set foot on other than his native Earth. He landed on the moon.

The Isolation of the Races.

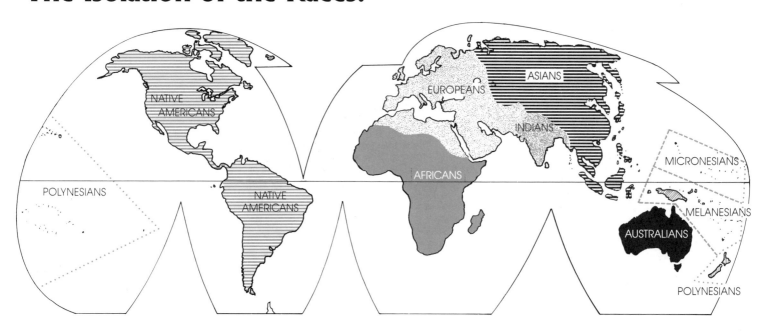

As modern humans spread across the globe, mountain ranges, deserts, and rising sea levels once again separated the various peoples. Alone, each group changed to better fit local conditions and local standards for attractiveness. Today scientists recognize as few as 5 or as many as 30 different races of humankind. Nevertheless, the differences remain so minor that every individual alive today still fits the description of the species, *Homo sapiens sapiens.*

Arctic humans tend to be chunky and short to hold heat. People of the desert tend to be slender to cool off more easily. Where food is scarce, humans are small so they will not need much food. Large humans live only where food is plentiful.

Some northern groups have lighter skin. This helps them absorb the seasonally reduced sunlight to produce the vitamins all humans need. Equatorial groups tend to be darker-skinned, which protects them from sunburn.

Asians are noted for the fold of skin around their eyes. It may have developed to protect them from glare and bitter winter winds. On the other hand, since similar eye folds also appear in such unrelated groups as the San people, Laplanders, and infant Euroamericans, the responsible gene may be primitive and universal to the species.

ASIAN EYE FOLD

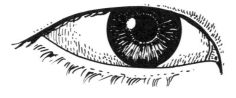

The races are divided chiefly according to geography.

South of the Sahara, Africans are dark-skinned with brown eyes, tightly coiled black hair, and thick lips.

In Africa north of the Sahara, in Europe, and in southwestern Asia, the people are light to dark-skinned, with curly to straight hair that may be colored black, red, blond, or brown. Some have blue, gray, green, or hazel eyes. People from India are related to Europeans but usually they have brown eyes, brown skin and black hair.

Asia from Siberia to Indonesia is home to people with yellow-brown skin and straight black hair. Many have eye folds and pads of fat over their cheekbones.

All Native Americans come from the Asian groups and share many similar features.

Native Australians have light to black skin, large teeth, and a narrow skull.

The islands of the South Pacific contain three distinct races. To the north, Micronesians have dark skin and wavy to wooly hair. Most of them are small. Around New Guinea, Melanesians have dark skin and are of medium stature. To the south, from New Zealand to Hawaii, Polynesians have light to brown skin and are usually tall and stout.

The isolation of the races came to an end when great conquerors spread war beyond their natural frontiers. The 1500s through 1800s brought shiploads of white Europeans and black Africans to the New World, as well as to many other parts of the globe. Today worldwide travel has made racial intermixing increasingly possible as a matter of choice, rather than force.

Human Evolution Today, Tomorrow, and Beyond.

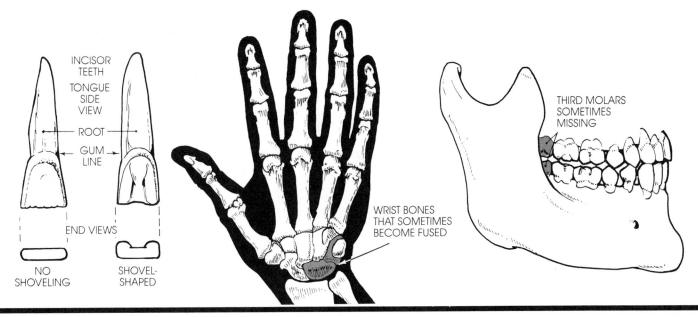

INCISOR TEETH
TONGUE SIDE VIEW
ROOT
GUM LINE
END VIEWS
NO SHOVELING
SHOVEL-SHAPED

WRIST BONES THAT SOMETIMES BECOME FUSED

THIRD MOLARS SOMETIMES MISSING

Evolution did not come to a screeching halt when humans appeared on this planet. Minor changes have already been noted in certain groups.

In most Asians and Native Americans, the backs of the incisors have extra ridges not found in other human teeth. Certain West Africans have one less bone in their wrist because two have become fused together. Many adults have only 28 teeth, not 32. The missing ones are the rearmost molars, or "wisdom teeth," absent in only 3 percent of some races, up to 70 percent in others.

What evolutionary changes does the future hold for humans? Long-term forecasting is as impossible to predict as the weather. Remember, evolution is a series of random trials and errors that either succeed in their time and place or don't. Nevertheless, the following trends have already become apparent.

Racial differences are blurring with worldwide travel on the upswing, and an increase in the acceptance of mixed families and societies.

Larger brains will once again be possible as the limitations of the birth

canal are overcome by cesarean sections (surgically removing the unborn baby from its mother).

Famine will hit hard unless birth-rates come down. All living things need some way to keep their numbers in check. Humans have done away with most of their natural ills and they have no natural enemies. Populations grow faster than the food supply. Famine then brings the death rate back in line with the birthrate.

In the past, new subspecies have appeared during ice-cap advances and retreats. The next Ice Age is due in about 20,000 years. Will that be when we finally see a new species of human?

What are the chances of finding humanlike life-forms on other planets? Not great. The chances seem to be much better that others will find us first. Perhaps they already have.

Considering the long history of Earth itself, what we will probably find on other planets is a peek into our own planet's past. Where life exists at all, it will probably be no more complex than bacteria. A few dozen planets in this galaxy will probably

contain multicellular organisms. Even fewer might contain large dinosaur-like organisms.

In its 4.5-billion-year history, the earth has supported speaking human beings for less than 50,000 years. That is only one-thousandth of 1 percent of the total time. Considering the twists and turns that evolution has taken to produce us, what are the odds of that happening again? Perhaps there is only one other planet in this entire galaxy with humanlike beings on it. If there is, then perhaps someday we will be able to compare our ancestry with theirs.

IS THIS A FUTURE HUMAN, AN EXAMPLE OF PARALLEL EVOLUTION ON ANOTHER PLANET, OR PURE IMAGINATION?

A Summary of Skeletal Evolution in Lobe-fin Fish and Early

The bony skeleton in human ancestry first appears as an external skeleton of (1) interconnected scales and (2) head plates, and an internal skeleton consisting of (3) a jointed braincase, (4) gill bars, and (5) disconnected elements surrounding the notochord. (6) Teeth rim the edge of the jaws. (7) Fangs descend from the forepart of the braincase.

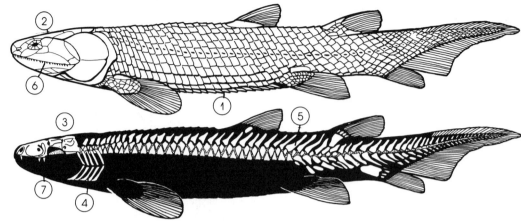

OSTEOLEPIS EXTERNAL AND INTERNAL VIEWS

In adapting to life on land, the following changes occur: (1) The body flattens. (2) Dorsal and (3) anal fins disappear. (4) Ribs appear. (5) Jointed bones appear in the muscular fins. (6) Jawline deepens as (7) the gill covers shrink. (8) Nostrils face downward. (9) Eyes migrate to top of skull. (10) Scales become smaller and more numerous.

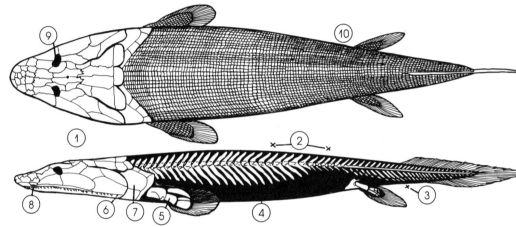

PANDERICHTHYS EXTERNAL VIEW OF TOP AND INTERNAL VIEW OF SIDE

The first tetrapod has (1) legs, ankle-bones, and (2) five jointed digits. (3) Fin rays are absent on the legs. (4) Eardrum notch appears. (5) Gill covers shrink. (6) Shoulder girdle enlarges and disconnects from skull, (7) Ribs develop large overlapping plates. (8) Vertebrae interconnect. (9) Pelvis enlarges and connects to one pair of ribs. (10) Tail lengthens. (11) Tail fin shrinks.

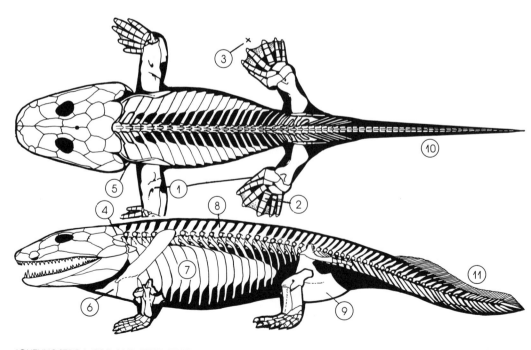

ICHTHYOSTEGA TOP AND SIDE VIEWS

Tetrapods.

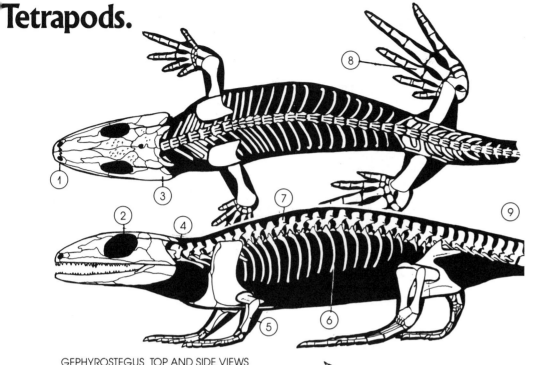

GEPHYROSTEGUS TOP AND SIDE VIEWS

Land-dwelling amphibians have the following adaptations: (1) Nostrils migrate to tip of snout. (2) Eyes enlarge and (3) skull squares off. (4) Neck appears. (5) Limbs become thinner. (6) Rib plates disappear. (7) Each vertebra solidifies as notochord shrinks to a thread and disks. (8) Feet become larger. (9) Tail fin, gill covers, and lateral-line canals are all absent in adults.

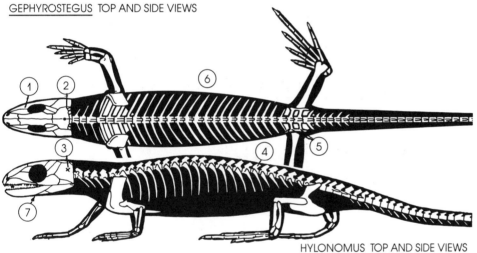

HYLONOMUS TOP AND SIDE VIEWS

The first reptiles display the following changes: (1) Smaller skull (2) without table horns or (3) eardrum notches. (4) Stronger backbone with notochord reduced to disks only. (5) Pelvis attaches to two pairs of ribs. (6) Shape becomes more slender overall. (7) Palate fangs disappear but back-of-palate teeth appear.

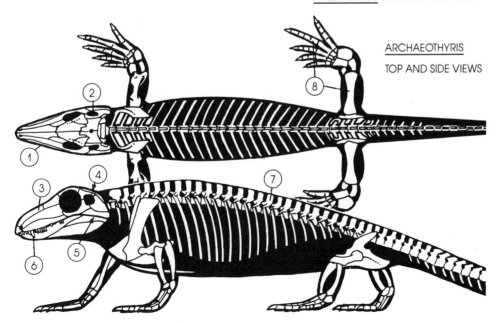

ARCHAEOTHYRIS

TOP AND SIDE VIEWS

Remains of early synapsids show the following: (1) Larger skull with (2) new opening in cheek/temple region. (3) Larger snout develops. (4) The downslope at the rear of the skull (5) is matched by the slope of the jawline. (6) Large canines appear. (7) Larger vertebrae support larger body. (8) Larger limbs and shorter toes appear.

A Summary of Skeletal Evolution in Early Synapsids.

Meat-eating early synapsids (pelycosaurs) display the following characteristics: (1) Longer teeth (especially canines) with flatter blades. (2) Jawline develops "grinning" curve. (3) Rear jaw bone develops thin flange. (4) Claws enlarge. (5) Limbs become longer. (6) Three pairs of ribs attach to pelvis.

The earliest therapsids have the following modifications: (1) Longer snout. (2) Larger upper canines. (3) Rear jaw flange enlarged and thinner. (4) Narrower shoulder blades that "float" over ribs. (5) More slender limbs. (6) Digits all more nearly the same size as some joints shrink. (7) Enlarged third eye.

Later meat-eating therapsids show the following changes: (1) Larger temple openings. (2) Smaller third eye. (3) Larger lower canines. (4) Larger tooth-bearing jawbone, with upward flange. (5) Elbows-back, knees-forward stance. (6) Ribs shorten in lower back. (7) Tail shortens.

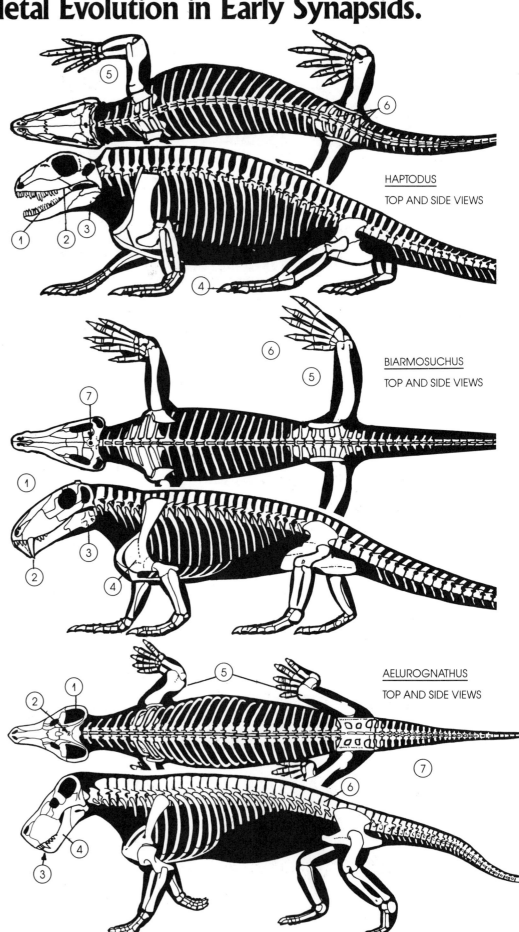

HAPTODUS
TOP AND SIDE VIEWS

BIARMOSUCHUS
TOP AND SIDE VIEWS

AELUROGNATHUS
TOP AND SIDE VIEWS

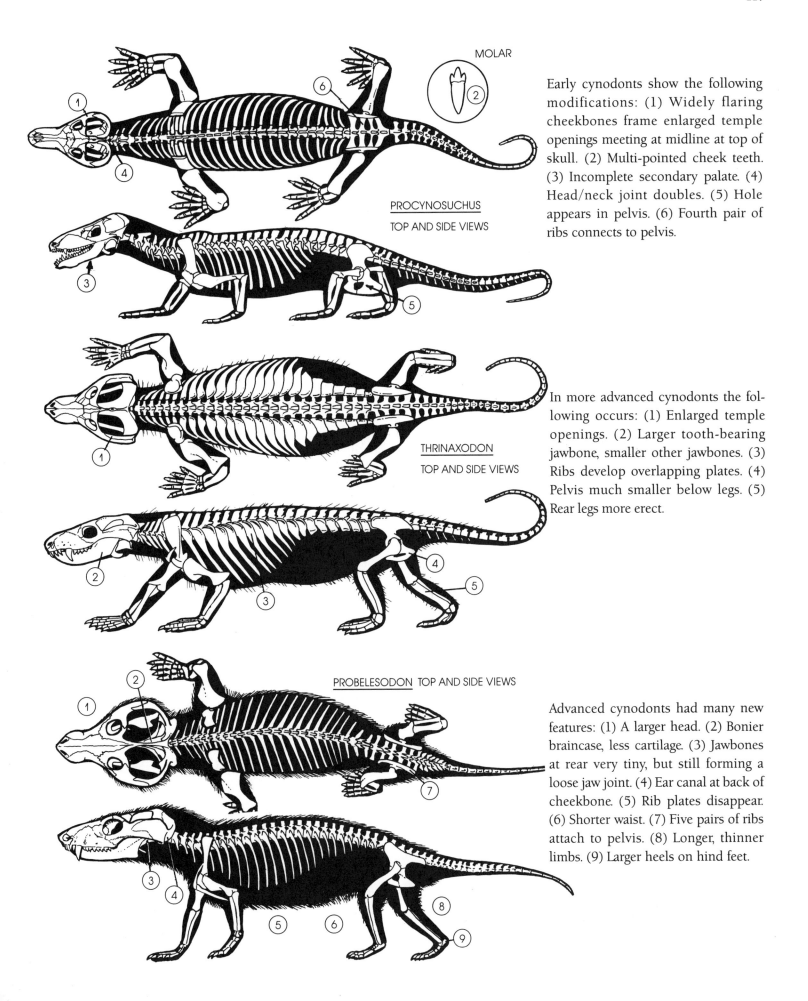

MOLAR

PROCYNOSUCHUS
TOP AND SIDE VIEWS

THRINAXODON
TOP AND SIDE VIEWS

PROBELESODON TOP AND SIDE VIEWS

Early cynodonts show the following modifications: (1) Widely flaring cheekbones frame enlarged temple openings meeting at midline at top of skull. (2) Multi-pointed cheek teeth. (3) Incomplete secondary palate. (4) Head/neck joint doubles. (5) Hole appears in pelvis. (6) Fourth pair of ribs connects to pelvis.

In more advanced cynodonts the following occurs: (1) Enlarged temple openings. (2) Larger tooth-bearing jawbone, smaller other jawbones. (3) Ribs develop overlapping plates. (4) Pelvis much smaller below legs. (5) Rear legs more erect.

Advanced cynodonts had many new features: (1) A larger head. (2) Bonier braincase, less cartilage. (3) Jawbones at rear very tiny, but still forming a loose jaw joint. (4) Ear canal at back of cheekbone. (5) Rib plates disappear. (6) Shorter waist. (7) Five pairs of ribs attach to pelvis. (8) Longer, thinner limbs. (9) Larger heels on hind feet.

A Summary of Skeletal Evolution in Mammals.

The first mammals show the following changes: (1) The nostrils merge to form one hole. (2) No bone surrounds the eye socket. (3) Cheekbone more slender. (4) Much larger braincase. (5) Enlarged tooth-bearing jawbone forms new jaw joint. (6) Neck bones compressed. (7) High arch to backbone. (8) Lower backbone without ribs. (9) Marsupial bones probably appear. (10) Top of pelvis disappears, except in front of leg socket. (11) Molars with twin roots.

MEGAZOSTRODON TOP AND SIDE VIEWS

MOLAR

SKULL OF MORGANUCODON

Living tree shrews have many primitive characteristics yet display the following advances: (1) Bone once again surrounds eye socket. (2) Brain much enlarged. (3) Shoulder blades broader and with central ridge. (4) Elbows tucked in at sides. (5) Longer tail. (6) Marsupial bones absent. (7) Digits able to grasp.

TREE SHREW TOP AND SIDE VIEWS

Most primates are tree climbers with the following traits: (1) Longer limbs and digits. (2) On the feet, the big toes diverge from the others. (3) The eyes face forward. (4) Body larger overall, except skull.

NOTHARCTUS TOP AND SIDE VIEWS

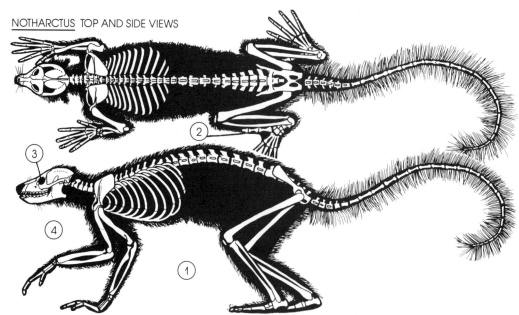

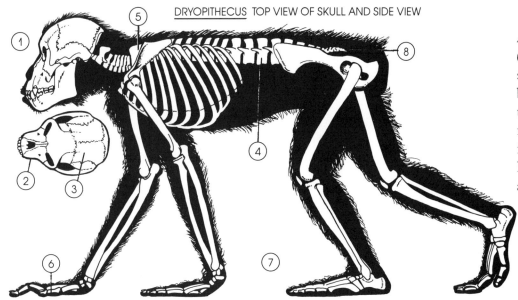

DRYOPITHECUS TOP VIEW OF SKULL AND SIDE VIEW

Apes present the following features: (1) A larger skull with (2) a short snout, and (3) larger braincase. (4) The backbone is shorter and stiffer, but (5) the shoulders and other arm joints are more flexible. (6) The thumb diverges from the other digits. (7) All digits have nails, not claws. (8) The tail is absent.

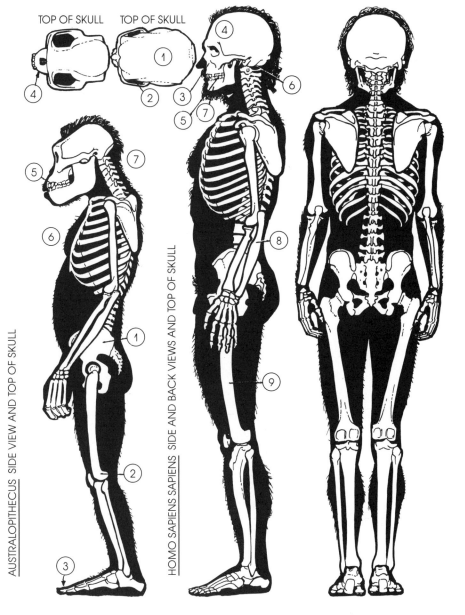

TOP OF SKULL   TOP OF SKULL

AUSTRALOPITHECUS SIDE VIEW AND TOP OF SKULL

HOMO SAPIENS SAPIENS SIDE AND BACK VIEWS AND TOP OF SKULL

Hominids walk erect with the following adaptations: (1) Pelvis shorter and broader. (2) Legs knock-kneed beneath body. (3) Big toe no longer diverges but works together with other digits. (4) Snout reduced. (5) Smaller canines, larger molars. (6) Chest wider than deep. (7) Neck inserts below skull.

Humans have the following new features: (1) Enlarged braincase. (2) Reduced temple openings. (3) Reduced snout. (4) Prominent forehead. (5) Smaller teeth. (6) Head balanced on neck. (7) Chin appears as jaws shrink. (8) Shorter arms. (9) Longer legs.

The Evolution of the Human Jaw and Ear Bones—the best

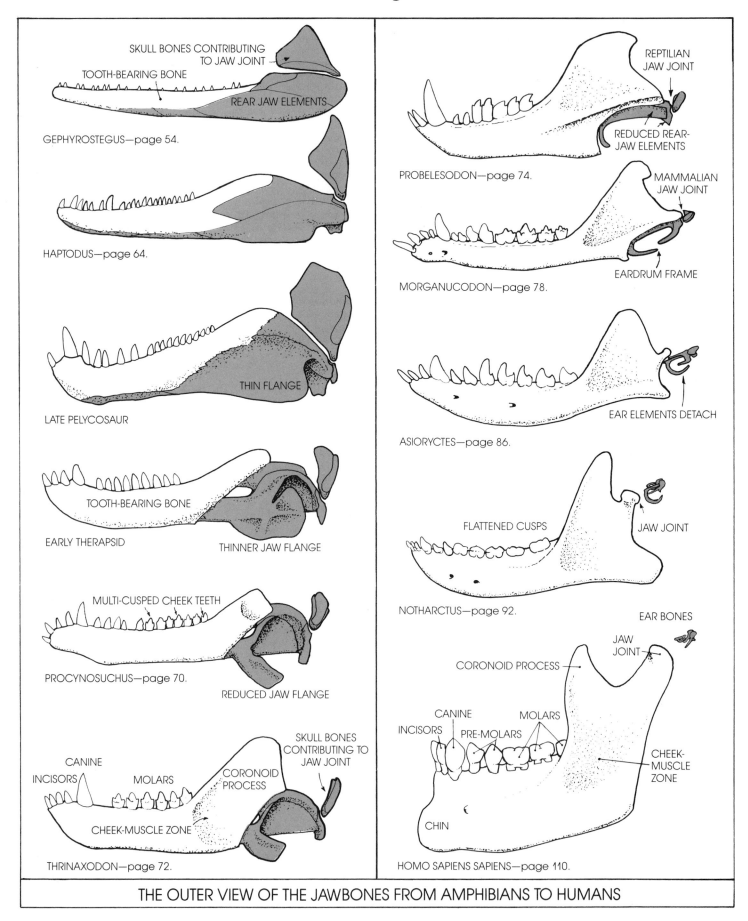

SKULL BONES CONTRIBUTING TO JAW JOINT

TOOTH-BEARING BONE

REAR JAW ELEMENTS

GEPHYROSTEGUS—page 54.

HAPTODUS—page 64.

THIN FLANGE

LATE PELYCOSAUR

TOOTH-BEARING BONE

EARLY THERAPSID

THINNER JAW FLANGE

MULTI-CUSPED CHEEK TEETH

PROCYNOSUCHUS—page 70.

REDUCED JAW FLANGE

CANINE

INCISORS   MOLARS

CORONOID PROCESS

SKULL BONES CONTRIBUTING TO JAW JOINT

CHEEK-MUSCLE ZONE

THRINAXODON—page 72.

REPTILIAN JAW JOINT

REDUCED REAR-JAW ELEMENTS

PROBELESODON—page 74.

MAMMALIAN JAW JOINT

EARDRUM FRAME

MORGANUCODON—page 78.

EAR ELEMENTS DETACH

ASIORYCTES—page 86.

FLATTENED CUSPS

JAW JOINT

NOTHARCTUS—page 92.

EAR BONES

JAW JOINT

CORONOID PROCESS

CANINE   MOLARS

INCISORS   PRE-MOLARS

CHEEK-MUSCLE ZONE

CHIN

HOMO SAPIENS SAPIENS—page 110.

THE OUTER VIEW OF THE JAWBONES FROM AMPHIBIANS TO HUMANS

example of gradual change in evolution.

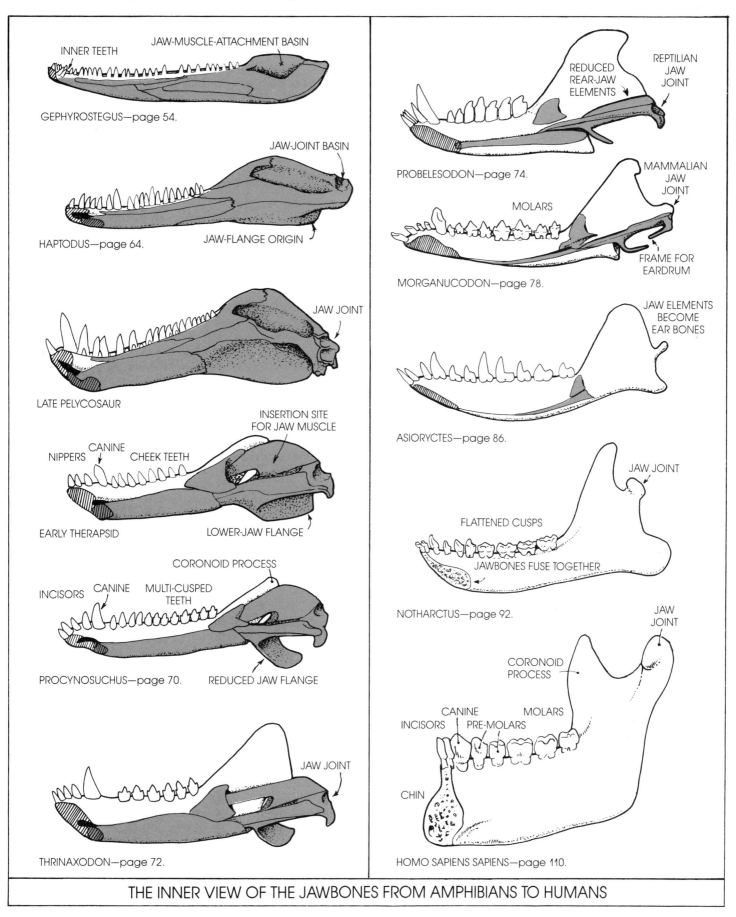

GEPHYROSTEGUS—page 54.

INNER TEETH

JAW-MUSCLE-ATTACHMENT BASIN

HAPTODUS—page 64.

JAW-JOINT BASIN

JAW-FLANGE ORIGIN

LATE PELYCOSAUR

JAW JOINT

EARLY THERAPSID

INSERTION SITE FOR JAW MUSCLE

NIPPERS   CANINE   CHEEK TEETH

LOWER-JAW FLANGE

PROCYNOSUCHUS—page 70.

CORONOID PROCESS

INCISORS   CANINE   MULTI-CUSPED TEETH

REDUCED JAW FLANGE

THRINAXODON—page 72.

JAW JOINT

PROBELESODON—page 74.

REDUCED REAR-JAW ELEMENTS

REPTILIAN JAW JOINT

MORGANUCODON—page 78.

MAMMALIAN JAW JOINT

MOLARS

FRAME FOR EARDRUM

ASIORYCTES—page 86.

JAW ELEMENTS BECOME EAR BONES

NOTHARCTUS—page 92.

FLATTENED CUSPS

JAWBONES FUSE TOGETHER

JAW JOINT

HOMO SAPIENS SAPIENS—page 110.

JAW JOINT

CORONOID PROCESS

INCISORS   CANINE   MOLARS

PRE-MOLARS

CHIN

THE INNER VIEW OF THE JAWBONES FROM AMPHIBIANS TO HUMANS

The Face of Humans, Prehumans, and their Ancestors.

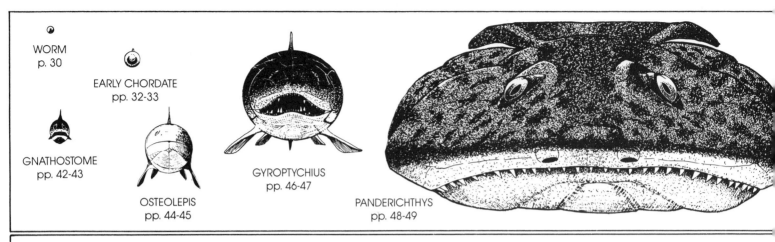

WORM
p. 30

EARLY CHORDATE
pp. 32-33

GNATHOSTOME
pp. 42-43

OSTEOLEPIS
pp. 44-45

GYROPTYCHIUS
pp. 46-47

PANDERICHTHYS
pp. 48-49

NOTHARCTUS
pp. 92-93

TREE SHREW
pp. 88-89

ASIORYCTES
pp. 86-87

MEGAZOSTRODON
pp. 78-81

PACHYGENELUS
pp. 76-77

PROBELESODON
pp. 74-75

AEGYPTOPITHECUS
pp. 94-95

DRYOPITHECUS
pp. 96-97

AUSTRALOPITHECUS
pp. 102-105

Illustrations are 60 percent of life size.

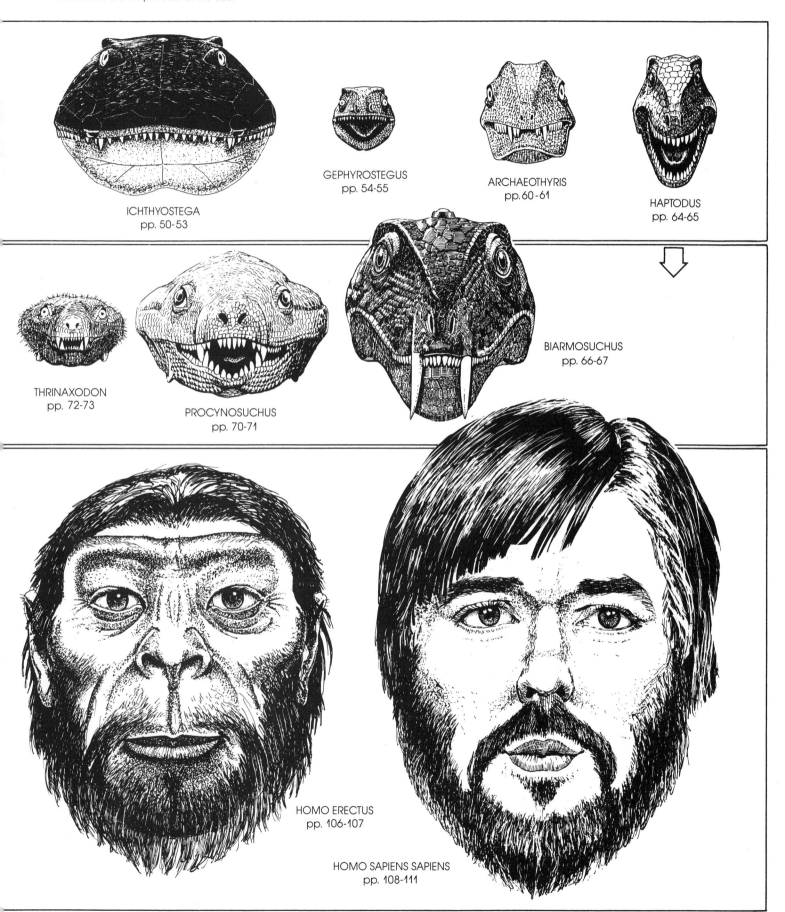

ICHTHYOSTEGA
pp. 50-53

GEPHYROSTEGUS
pp. 54-55

ARCHAEOTHYRIS
pp. 60-61

HAPTODUS
pp. 64-65

THRINAXODON
pp. 72-73

PROCYNOSUCHUS
pp. 70-71

BIARMOSUCHUS
pp. 66-67

HOMO ERECTUS
pp. 106-107

HOMO SAPIENS SAPIENS
pp. 108-111

Recommended Reading

For those wishing to learn more about human evolution or prehistoric animals, I suggest the following books:

General

Grizmek's Encyclopedia of Evolution. The articles by W. F. Gutmann (on chordate evolution) and H. Wendt (on microorganisms and the origins of life) are especially helpful.

Microorganisms and the Origin of Life

Margulis, Lynn, and Dorion Sagan. *Microcosmos.* New York: Summit Books, 1986.

Woese, Carl. "Archebacteria," in *Scientific American* 6/1981.

Vertebrate Evolution

Carroll, Robert L. *Vertebrate Paleontology and Evolution.* New York: W. H. Freeman & Co., 1987.

Romer, Alfred S. *The Vertebrate Body—Shorter Version.* Philadelphia: W. B. Saunders Co., 1971.

Savage, R. J. G., and M. R. Long. *Mammal Evolution, An Illustrated Guide.* New York: Facts on File, 1986; London: The British Museum (Natural History).

Primates and Tree Shrews

Ciochon, Russell L., and John G. Fleagle. *Primate Evolution and Human Origins.* Menlo Park, CA: The Benjamin-Cummings Publishing Co., 1985.

Clark, Wilfred E. *The Antecedents of Man.* New York: Quadrangle Books, 1971.

Rosen, S. I. *Introduction to the Primates, Living and Fossil.* Englewood Cliffs, NJ: Prentice-Hall, 1974.

Szalay, F. S., and E. Delson. *Evolutionary History of the Primates.* San Diego, CA: Academic Press, 1979.

Index